ENDORSEMENTS

"*According to His Purpose* is a God given, very clear manuscript. It makes the complicated simple and has been a perfect help to me. The book is really, really wonderful. Dr. Cobbin, you have truly blessed me. Keep up the great work!"

– Dr. Nora Hutto, Dean-School of Education, 2011
The University of St. Thomas, Houston, Texas

"This book is a reflection of the depth of love and commitment Dr. Jacqueline Cobbin has for our Lord. Dr. Cobbin has masterfully laid out principles inside these pages that if placed into motion, will help one to recognize the full potential of his/her life. She directs us to realize that our lives can be rewarding, significant and more fruitful than we ever thought or dreamed. Our lives can be transformed to unleash hidden potential to reveal a life that is big, bigger than you could ever dream; into one you'll love and praise God for the making."

– Kathy Burrell, Prayer Guild Honoree - College of Biblical Studies
Pastor George E. Burrell, Sr., Internal Hope Fellowship Church

"Be encouraged! Dr. Cobbin inspires us with a stirring narrative of hope and courage. We are all made in the image of our Heavenly Father, and no matter what challenges we may face in this life, the Lord has given us His Power to overcome them and to fulfill our God-given purpose!"

– Kim Orr, Associate Pastor and Director of Christian Education
Windsor Village United Methodist Church

"From the moment Dr. Cobbin shared that is was illegal to die before completing ones purpose, I was convinced. I WILL NOT DIE A CROOK! This life-long educator has written a book that shares her heart and love for The Lord in ways that are inspirational and motivational. It's one thing to know that God has a purpose for us. Learning to become what He has called us to become can require a little coaching. Dr. Cobbin is the perfect mentor. *According To His Purpose* has elevated me to another level of thinking about the value of my life and the lives of all the folk around me. There's a Tweet-worthy phrase in every chapter of the book.

Among my favorites: *"Hearing from God is a spiritual privilege. When you extend an invitation to Him to join you in conversation, His response is a gift."* This book is a gift!"

– Irv White, Associate Pastor and Director of Marketing
Windsor Village United Methodist Church

"While reading *According To His Purpose* I found this book to be impactful, encouraging, inspiring, and easy to read. Dr. Cobbin gives easy to apply instructions, that I feel compel you to passionately pursue God's purpose for your life. She clearly details what purpose is, its importance and how not to abort God's purpose for your life. Dr. Cobbin's transparency is refreshing as she instructs Christians to come out of the closet and become the disciples the world needs. Her statement, *"Show me your friends and I'll show you your future",* is profound! If you are ready to live according to God's purpose, I strongly recommend that you read this book."

– Jeanette Allen, Author/ CEO, Women's Ministries
Windsor Village United Methodist Church

"*According to His Purpose* has clearly laid out Dr. Cobbin's approach and presented it in very manageable segments which will appeal both to Christians and persons seeking their own individual purpose everywhere. Dr. Cobbin demonstrates the love of God in her personal life and testimony, to her Church, Community and even to the far ends of the Earth in Kenya. According to Acts 1:8. Her great love for people permeates this book and gives us all hope, even in the darkest of seasons. Reading *According to His Purpose* will bring you peace in the midst of all seasons of life and teach you how to keep the faith in times of testing."

–Velosia Kibe, Associate Pastor
and Director of KBC Orphanage-Kenya
Windsor Village United Methodist Church

ACCORDING TO  HIS PURPOSE

DR. JACQUELINE HORTON-COBBIN

EVERFAITH PRESS

Cover & Interior Design by D.E. West - ZAQ Designs

Printed in the United States of America.

www.everfaithpress.com

TABLE of CONTENTS

CONTENTS

FOREWORD

Committed to His Purpose

*E*very morning and several times a day I study and *meditate on God's word. This book has become a part of that meditation. Even though I have already lived more years than promised, this book helps me to understand that God continues to have an ordained-purpose for my life in this "season."*

– Dr. Rod Paige, U.S. Secretary of Education (2001-2005)

*T*he two most important days in your life is when you *were born and the day you understand God's purpose for your life and then start to walk in that purpose. This book invokes meditation, prayer and brings you closer to that understanding. We thank Jesus for allowing you to be apart our lives, Dr. Cobbin.*

– Stephanie Nellons-Paige, Business Executive

Awakened to His Purpose

*A*ccording *To His Purpose* is an enthralling piece of literally work that not only provides sincere spiritual guidance but one that gives a detailed blueprint of how to pave and achieve a path of success in life through Christ. From the moment I read the first word of the book to the very last word I could not lay the book down, for even a minute. It is a powerful literary work that will change the lives of many.

This book and Dr. Jacqueline Cobbin have tremendously impacted my life, as I am a product of her tutoring since 5th grade after she rescued me from special education classes upon moving to the United States from India. It has truly been an honor to have gained an understanding from Dr. Cobbin about the power on spiritual and intellectual knowledge. According to His Purpose is a fresh reminder to me that God is alive, always there when times get tough and that waiting patiently on God, while remembering that He is in control are the true keys to success.

– Steven Mathew John, Graduating Senior
Bauer College of Business
The University of Houston

INTRODUCTION

We All Have a Purpose in Life

During a Prayer Explosion at Windsor Village United Methodist Church, Pastor Isaac Petre blew our minds when he said, "It is illegal to die before you complete your purpose." This statement resonated with me a great deal because I have been on a spiritual trajectory toward fulfilling my purpose most of my life. I knew that I was called "according to His purpose" as I watched its beautiful manifestation in the various seasons in my life.

My journey started as a child. My mother was very precise in her molding me to be a leader and an educator. She distinctly knew my gifts and calling, and prepared a life plan for my success. I was encouraged to take leadership positions in church, school activities, and in the community. She taught me the nuances of what a lady does and doesn't do and heavily influenced me to carry myself

accordingly. Thus, Pastor Petre's revelation had been the genesis for my life development even before I heard his words that night.

He referenced Ecclesiastes 3:1, "There is a time for everything, and a season for every activity under the heavens…" When I, Jacqueline Pryor, was born, God strategically placed me on the earth for "such a time as this" with His purpose for my life securely downloaded into my DNA. The same applies to your life. You have a divine purpose that must be fulfilled during this lifetime for the glory of God's kingdom. *It is illegal to die before you complete your purpose.*

The Master Creator created everything in the book of Genesis for the glory of His kingdom. That includes you, man, and woman. He was so pleased with His creation that in Genesis 1, He says, "And God saw that it was good" five times. Then He concludes the chapter with this statement in Genesis 1:31: "And God saw everything that He had made, and, behold, it was very good." You are God's masterpiece, the apple of His eye. He loved you so much that He entrusted you to represent His kingdom here on earth and gave you a divine assignment to fulfill to forward His kingdom, bringing others into the kingdom.

Why write another book on fulfilling God's purpose? There are at least thousands out there already that thor-

oughly address the issue. Well, most of those books focus on fulfilling your purpose outside of church walls, whereas this book focuses on the importance of showing up for God, in the "season," He has ordained, how to do that effectively, and the consequences of life when you don't.

A season is an appropriate occasion for harvesting. In my context, a season is when you have a date with destiny! Your purpose is your God-assignment, and there is a field out there called "the world" that is ready for harvest. You've got to get out into the field to get your harvest, particularly when God has made that your primary focus. If you are a Christian, Christ reminds us in Matthew 28:18–20 of our Christian mandate:

Then Jesus came to them and said, "All authority in heaven and on earth has been given to me. *Therefore go and make disciples of all nations, baptizing them in the name of the Father and of the Son and of the Holy Spirit, and teaching them to obey everything I have commanded you.* And surely I am with you always, to the very end of the age."

You can bet that your purpose is tied into that mandate. As an ambassador for the kingdom of God, who is called, equipped, and empowered to fulfill your purpose, it's imperative for you to be headed in the right direc-

tion. This book will help you get there if you have not already started the journey.

We all go through seasons, and we have a very definitive purpose in each one of those seasons. Your purpose is your cause, your reason for existing! Your cause is the reason why you were born.

Right now you are reading this book because you are either about to do something *fabulous* for God, need encouragement to pursue your purpose, or need to be realigned with your purpose. We are going to take a magnifying glass called the Holy Spirit and determine what your purpose is in this season of your life and for the rest of your life. I am absolutely assured that you will be able to take something away from this journey that will empower you for the glory of God's kingdom, now and forevermore, **According to His Purpose**.

CHAPTER 1

Defining God's Purpose

"For I know the plans I have for you," declares the Lord, "plans to prosper you and not to harm you, plans to give you hope and a future." (Jeremiah 29:11)

God, the Master Creator, designed you with a unique purpose in mind. So if someone tells you you're not special, you have irrefutable evidence that it's not true. You are so unique that no one on the face of the planet has your exact fingerprint. Considering that the world population was 7.125 billion in 2013, that's a lot of fingerprints. If God is such a stickler for details, perhaps you should be a stickler too when it comes to desiring to live your life according to His purpose. God has specifically left this note for you in Jeremiah 29:11 outlining the fact that He has a distinct plan for your life. It is up to you to find out what that is so that you can fulfill it while here on earth.

DEFINING GOD'S PURPOSE

We have established that all of mankind is born into this world with a purpose in mind. Since God is the Creator, He knows which purpose is best for us. It is very important that we become believers in Christ in order to be able to hear His voice instructing us on what that purpose is and how to fulfill it in our lifetime. Knowing that each of us has the ability to hear from God in regards to that purpose is empowering. We must intentionally listen for what He has prepared for us to do. We have all been assigned a divine place for kingdom purpose, be it our church, our school, or our profession. It is our responsibility to *be* what God has called us to be in that place, regardless of what we may find when we get there. As we are assigned to that place, then we must follow God's plan for us, using a dialogue with Him to make our decisions while also taking into consideration the circumstances of the place that we find ourselves. If we keep all of this in mind, then we are able to clearly understand that our purpose in life is actually what God made us and called us to be, in a particular place, with certain circumstances, allowing us to be a blessing not only to the body of Christ, but also to glorify God. Whether we accept the mission or not is contained in the free will that God has given each of us.

Proverbs 4:7 (KJV) says, "Wisdom is the principal thing; therefore get wisdom: and with all thy getting get understanding." That is what we all should be striving for: wisdom. What is wisdom? Wisdom is the true understanding of the voice of God. If we know that with wisdom we get understanding, then wisdom is what each one of us should be striving to achieve in order to gain the unique understanding of our Christian walk.

Getting a clear understanding of what God is requiring us to do is imperative to our development as Christians. I can remember instances early on in life, where I wanted to do something else and started on the pathway to my chosen profession. As a young girl, I wanted to be a secular singer, and to do other things that did not glorify God such as sing in night clubs, go to Hollywood, and become a star. This was not what God had for me to do; instead, I was blessed to receive a music scholarship to attend college and pursue a career that would glorify God. I became an educator.

WHO IS GOD AND HOW DOES MY PURPOSE FIT INTO HIS PLAN FOR MY LIFE?

Many have been taught that God is really a Godhead, or Trinity, made up of the Father, Son, and the Holy Spirit.

If we have been born again in Christ and we understand that we are His children, and we realize that the Holy Spirit speaks to us and the Bible is our instruction manual, then we know what is said in Proverbs 3:5–6 is actually true. The Scripture states, "Trust in the Lord with all your heart and lean not on your own understanding; in all your ways submit to him, and he will make your paths straight." God is calling for us to submit all of who we are to Him so that we can walk in the fullness of His purpose for our lives. Knowing that we can do this, He has declared that "the way" to Him is through His Son, Jesus Christ. If you are a born again believer and have accepted Jesus Christ as your Lord and Savior, then you have made a commitment to allow Him to be Lord (someone who has *full* authority) over you. When someone who has authority over you establishes a plan for your life, your desire should be to seek further instruction. Submission to the Lordship of Jesus Christ is compulsory, yet we do it not because we have to, but because He first loved us. Our love for Him compels us to render a reciprocal response. Simply speaking, we seek His purpose for our lives because we love Him.

Let's look at Romans 8:14–17; it gives us a clearer picture of our relationship with God and the Trinity.

For those who are led by the Spirit of God
are the children of God. The Spirit you received

does not make you slaves, so that you live in fear again; rather, the Spirit you received brought about your adoption to sonship. And by him we cry, "Abba, Father." The Spirit himself testifies with our spirit that we are God's children. Now if we are children, then we are heirs—heirs of God and co-heirs with Christ, if indeed we share in his sufferings in order that we may also share in his glory.

Knowing that we are the children of God is amazing, but being coheirs to Jesus' heavenly inheritance is one of the greatest benefits in our Christian walk. He promised us that as we serve God, using His example as a blueprint, we could have abundant life now. He also said that the benefits would come with trials and tribulation, but that we could have a portion of that heavenly inheritance right here on earth if we committed our lives to be ambassadors for the kingdom of God.

The other benefit of walking in God's purpose is the Godly confidence that grows or develops in us as we serve God with our whole hearts. When our will is lined up with God's will, there is a "sweetness" that fills our souls which enables us to walk in the fullness of Christ. The Bible describes this in Colossians 1:27 as walking in "the hope of glory."

HOW DO WE ACCESS GOD TO FIND
OUT WHAT OUR PURPOSE IS?

Once we have established Jesus Christ as our Lord and Savior, we have access to the Heavenly Father in His name. We pray and ask the Father what our purpose is, and He gladly answers us. If you have not received Jesus Christ as your Lord and Savior, there is a prayer at the end of the chapter that you can pray in order to do so. A good place to start is with the model prayer, the Lord's Prayer. Throughout the book, we will reference this prayer as a model for accessing God. Matthew 6:9–13 says:

Our Father, which art in heaven,
Hallowed be thy Name.
Thy Kingdom come.
Thy will be done in earth,
As it is in heaven.
Give us this day our daily bread.
And forgive us our trespasses,
As we forgive them that trespass against us.
And lead us not into temptation,
But deliver us from evil.
For thine is the kingdom,
The power, and the glory,
Forever and ever.
Amen.

When we petition the heart of God for His will to be done in our lives, we are asking Him to empower us to fulfill our divine purpose for the glory of His kingdom. As a kingdom ambassador, you have particular rights, and one of those rights allows you to have access to God, twenty-four hours a day, seven days a week. Prayer is the most common mode of communication for man or woman to talk with their heavenly Father.

God also uses the Holy Spirit to instruct us. He communicates with us concerning the things of God and gives us direction, correction, comfort, exhortation, and power to fulfill God's purpose for our lives. John 3:16 says that God loved us so much that He sent Jesus to be a sinless sacrifice for a sin-filled world. God's original intention was for man to fellowship with Him in the Garden of Eden. He has always desired to have a relationship with His creation. When Adam sinned, he fractured that relationship, and God then sent Jesus to pay the ultimate price for the sins of the world, once and for all. Jesus then sent the Holy Spirit as our Paraclete (Helper) to enable us to be successful in fulfilling our God-mission. What an elaborate plan for the redemption of man! Only a loving God could restore us to "right" relationship with Him and make us ambassadors here on earth, empowering us according to His purpose for His glory here on earth.

As promised, here is a prayer for salvation. The first critical step in living according to His purpose is to accept Jesus as your Lord and Savior. I commend you for taking this step today.

THE SALVATION PRAYER

Dear God in heaven, I come to you in the name of Jesus. I acknowledge to You that I am a sinner, and I am sorry for my sins and the life that I have lived; I need and ask for Your forgiveness.

I believe that Your only begotten Son, Jesus Christ, shed His precious blood on the cross at Calvary and died for my sins, and I am now willing to turn from my sins.

You said in Your Holy Word, in Romans 10:9 that if we confess the Lord our God and believe in our hearts that God raised Jesus from the dead, we shall be saved.

Right now I confess Jesus as the Lord of my soul. With my heart, I believe that God raised Jesus from the dead. This very moment I accept Jesus Christ as my own personal Savior, and according to His Word, right now I am saved.

Thank you, Jesus, for Your unlimited grace which has saved me from my sins. I thank You, Jesus, that Your grace never leads to license to sin, but rather always leads to repentance. Therefore, Lord Jesus, transform my life so that I may bring glory and honor to You alone.

Thank you, Jesus, for dying for me and giving me eternal life. Amen.[1]

Welcome to the body of Christ!

Chapter One Questions:

DEFINING GOD'S PURPOSE

1. How would you define God's purpose for your life?
2. What are the benefits of defining God's purpose for your life?
3. What do you see as God's purpose for mankind? How do you see yourself fitting into that purpose?
4. How will you access God to find out what your purpose is or do you instinctively know what it is?
5. State what your divine purpose is and/or use this time to ask God for direction in seeking His purpose for your life.

CHAPTER 2

Is Our Purpose "Doing" or Is It "Being"?

"By myself I can do nothing; I judge only as I hear,
and my judgment is just, for I seek not to please myself
but Him who sent me." (John 5:30)

When you accept Jesus Christ as your Lord and Savior, something divine happens in your DNA. You are awakened to your God-purpose! This rebirthing experience is akin to literally being regenerated to God's original intent for your life before the fall of man in the Garden of Eden. That is the "being" part of the divine equation. You are a human being fulfilling the divine call of God on your life, doing what He has predestined you to do before you were formed in your mother's womb.

Jesus said in John 5:30 that He could "do" nothing of himself. In other words, His power was bound to the will

of His Father. He only "did" what He was instructed to do by God, therefore His judgment was not impaired because He received His instructions straight from heaven. When you seek God with all your heart concerning your purpose, He is obligated to show you the way to do His will on the earth. Let's take a second glance at the Model Prayer:

> *Our Father, which art in heaven,*
> *Hallowed be thy Name.*
> *Thy Kingdom come.*
> *Thy will be done in earth,*
> *As it is in heaven.*
> *Give us this day our daily bread.*
> *And forgive us our trespasses,*
> *As we forgive them that trespass against us.*
> *And lead us not into temptation,*
> *But deliver us from evil.*
> *For thine is the kingdom,*
> *The power, and the glory,*
> *For ever and ever.*
> *Amen.*

"Thy Kingdom come. Thy will be done in earth, As it is in heaven" is a clear indication that God's intention for the mandated will from His heavenly heart for all mankind is

that it be fulfilled here on earth. He uses human *beings* as heavenly ambassadors to complete this task. Our purpose in life begins with our being and doing His will, but He expects us to also do for others. It has been my experience that what you make happen for others, God makes happen for you.

However, God is a lover of human beings. He loves us for who we are, not for what we do. His loving us is not predicated on what we do, but simply on who we are: His divine creation.

SEEKING TO HEAR
THE HEAVENLY FATHER'S VOICE

We live in a world of many voices. Making a deliberate attempt to listen for God's voice is so essential because there are so many voices and thoughts that are trying to control our mind. This is especially evident when we are seeking God's face and His voice. Many times it's important to seek God's voice in silence because the interruptions of life cause us to be in mental disarray, believing that we are hearing His voice when we are actually hearing the voice of others. Thus, discerning His voice amid the noise of everyday life must be a priority.

As children of God, sometimes we run around in circles trying to obey the various voices that are direct-

ing our lives without an understanding that it's His voice which allows us to be who we are meant to be. As a result of listening to other voices, our lives become so very fragmented. Sometimes destructive patterns or habits begin to creep into our lives, which keep us from being all that we are to be for God. Don't fall into the trap of listening to other voices, thinking that you've got to do so much to win God's love. It is your true heart that He looks at and your relationship with Him that are more meaningful than anything else.

It's important for us to walk closely with God and listen to Him. He gives us different directives in our quiet time with Him. His ultimate desire is for true companionship with us. Through our fellowship with God, we will be more apt to lift Him up rather than lifting up our circumstances. It is essential to know that God loves us for who we are, not for what we do. The doing comes after developing an honest and meaningful relationship with God based on who He has created us to be. When we understand that, our true purpose will be realized. In the next chapter, we will address how to be better able to discern God's voice.

"BEING" DISCIPLINED TO SEEK GOD

Our future is decided by the habits developed in our daily lives. God instructs us on how to establish effective

habits and in developing methodologies on how to "be" that lend themselves to kingdom success. You must remain open to God's instruction, as little children are on their first day in kindergarten. This is Jesus' response when asked who is the greatest in heaven:

> *He called a little child to Him, and placed the child among them. And He said: "'Truly I tell you, unless you change and become like little children, you will never enter the kingdom of heaven. Therefore, whoever takes the lowly position of this child is the greatest in the kingdom of heaven.'" (Matthew 18:2–4)*

In order to experience true kingdom success, you must remain teachable. In 1Corinthians 6:19–20, Paul stated, "Do you not know that your bodies are temples of the Holy Spirit, who is in you, whom you have received from God? You are not your own; you were bought at a price. Therefore honor God with your bodies." As a young adult, I had to be deliberate about establishing habits that would keep me in a position to hear God's instruction. He sometimes uses people, places, and things to get His message across. As a young woman, I was mentored by an older Christian woman by the name of Alberta Mitchell-

Caviel on how to maintain my temple so that I could do the work of the Lord. I started exercising and eating right under her leadership and treasuring a healthy lifestyle. When I was in my twenties, I was also inspired to read Stephen Covey's *The 7 Habits of Highly Effective People.* As a result, I am now able to continue to fulfill the calling God has on my life through a healthy lifestyle and habits well into my retirement years.

God also requires you to walk in love toward Him, yourself, and others on a daily basis no matter whether or not we are mistreated. We must always seek to behave in a manner that is becoming to our being children of the Most High God. That means always operating in love. We must love as Christ loved us. God loved us before we were even born into this world. Even knowing our sinful nature, He showed us the true meaning of love by forgiving us and accepting us just as we are. He has the right to judge us, but He chooses to look at us with nonjudgmental eyes. Thus, it is important for us, as followers of Christ, to walk in love and not be judgmental of others.

God also commands us not to be covetous, meaning that we should not be jealous, wanting what someone else has or being upset because our neighbor may have something that we believe we should have or some-

thing we desire. Often this starts occurring in our toddler years, when as young children we want a particular toy from another child. Then as we move from childhood to becoming a teenager, we may start looking at the physical attributes of someone else, wishing that we had been given a better nose or longer hair or were taller or shorter. All these are examples of the development of a covetous spirit.

God is also concerned about where we seek Him and the condition of our physical bodies when we do so. Imagine asking your earthly father for a gift or to share some valuable morsel of wisdom when you show up disheveled and reeking of filth. Imagine inviting him to your home for an engaging conversation, and he must wrestle with the smell of week old trash, battle with the loud, lewd conversation from a soap opera, and remove scattered laundry from your sofa in order to sit down for your discussion. Although this would not compromise his love for you, he would not be pleased. The same is true of God. We must properly prepare the atmosphere for His presence and eliminate anything that would be a distraction to our seeking Him.

Sometimes we are intimidated by the notion of having a conversation with God. Yet He isn't concerned so

much about how you say something, but about what you say. Foolish talking or making foolish gestures is an unacceptable mode of communication when talking to God. The old folks use to say, "The person who is talking the most is telling all the lies." If you are talking a lot, then most likely you aren't listening a whole lot to God. Frivolous conversation is an insult to Him. Ephesians 4:29 says, "Do not let any unwholesome talk come out of your mouths, but only what is helpful for building others up according to their needs, that it may benefit those who listen."Not only do you not want to talk foolishly, you don't want to commune with others who do it, as the Bible states, "Do not be misled: Bad company corrupts good character" (1 Corinthians 15:33).

We are inundated with reports of the daily occurrences in the lives of celebrities by the news media, on talk shows, and by gossip columnists on television and on social media. These celebrities have become demigods in our current society. This is just a snapshot of the things and people we worship in America today. We should not look at any man as an idol. The Scriptures tell us that God is a jealous God, and He does not want any man or thing placed over our allegiance to Him. As we walk in these daily routines and form these daily habits, we should walk

in love; we should not covet, not be filthy or operate in filth, not talk foolishly, or use foolish gestures. Otherwise, doing these things will result in negative consequences, and we will be dishonoring God.

Being disciplined to seek God is one thing; listening and obeying Him is another. Disobedience should not be a habit that you perpetuate in your daily routine. There are numerous accounts in the Bible where God's children were disobedient, and in not a single instance did it turn out well for them as a result. Why go through the trouble of seeking God without the intent of doing what He tells you to do? In order to walk according to His purpose, you must seek, obey, and love Him enough to fulfill your mission here on earth. 1 Samuel 15:22 says, "To obey is better than sacrifice, and to heed is better than the fat of rams." Establishing a daily routine that honors Him puts you in a position to reap the bountiful blessings that He has in store for you.

Being regenerated to the original intent for your life and doing things His way will make life so much more fulfilling as you live **According to His Purpose.**

'THE PRAYER FOR BEING WHAT GOD ORDAINED YOU TO BE

Heavenly Father of us all, holy is Your name. May Your will be done in my life so that I can become all that You have called me to become and do all that You direct me to do. Forgive me for doubting You and being disobedient. Deliver me from all that is evil and protect me as I pursue Your will. I make a fresh commitment to honor You in all that I do. In Jesus' name, Amen.

Chapter Two Questions:

IS OUR PURPOSE "DOING" OR IS IT "BEING?"

1. Now that you know what your purpose is, how will you implement it into your present being? If you are still seeking an answer from God, it is okay. (Think only about the implementation steps, here.)

2. How will you become what God wants you to become?

3. Is the power source (God Almighty) already within you? Can you turn on a switch to the Power Source through prayer and access God, listening for His answer?

4. Christ was "perfect." How can you be part of God's plan for His kingdom when you are not a spiritual super hero like Jesus?

CHAPTER 3

To Be or Not To Be?

""For in Him we live and move and have our being.'
As some of your own poets have said, 'We are
His offspring.'" (Acts 17:28)

We have established the fact that we are God's off-spring created in His very image. God made us to *be* the most important possession He has; therefore, embracing the truth about who God says you are is crucial.

Genesis 1:27 states, "So God created mankind in His own image, in the image of God He created them; male and female He created them." This truth and walking in its reality about whom and whose you are eradicates Satan's lie. He comes on a daily basis to steal, kill, and destroy this truth in your life.

Yet none of us are perfect, nor do we live a life free of concerns and challenges. We all face the same kinds of challenges and temptations, but by agreeing with God's vision for our lives, we can live in the reality of who God has made us to *be*. Each day we should deliberately choose to fulfill our Christian mandate to walk in the purpose that God has assigned us.

God has called each of us to exercise, within our sphere of influence, the unique gifts and talents He has given us. Be strong, be courageous, and be free to *be* all that God has called you to be. Remember Esther, the Jewish queen who won the heart of King Ahasuerus and save her people from complete annihilation by the evil noble Haman. Remember Harriet Tubman, the Black Moses of her generation, remembered throughout history for her heroic determination to get every slave who had the fortitude to do so flee from the tyranny of slavery through the Underground Railroad. We have numerous historical examples that have come before us, as well as a mighty army of kingdom women and men who have marched to the beat of God's drum. Ask God for courage to follow Him like these women and men did to accomplish your God-given mission.

HOW TO *BE*

The Holy Spirit introduces us to God. We cannot understand who God is and what He is truly about without the Holy Spirit. He teaches us about the things of God and how to posture ourselves for kingdom success.

Before we come to Christ, we have an unregenerated (unrenewed) mind. Even though God created us, because of the sin-nature of man, we walk after the dictates of the flesh. In other words, if we think it, we do it; if we want it, we get it. Our carnal flesh is in control of our lives, and our purpose is to fulfill the lust of the flesh, the lust of our eyes, and the pride in one's lifestyle. Whatever we hunger for or covet, that fuels our pursuit of a carnal purpose in life. But when we make a conscious decision to follow Jesus Christ and to accept His lordship over our lives, the Holy Spirit comes in and equips us to fulfill our kingdom purpose.

The first thing on His agenda is to clean up our stinking thinking. There's a parable in the New Testament where Jesus talks about the impossibility of putting "new wine" in "old wine skins." God's precious holy purpose for your life cannot be accomplished with your old mindset. Your mind must be renewed in the things of God. Your heart must follow and desire the things of God.

The Holy Spirit empowers us to accomplish our divine calling. Whatever that purpose is, which has been identified by God for our lives, the Holy Spirit equips us to achieve it.

Let's take an in-depth look at 1 Corinthians 2:9–16.

"What eye has seen, what no ear has heard, and what no human mind has conceived the things God has prepared for those who love him," these are the things God has revealed to us by his Spirit. The Spirit searches all things, even the deep things of God.

For who knows a person's thoughts except their own spirit within them? In the same way no one knows the thoughts of God except the Spirit of God. What we have received is not the spirit of the world, but the Spirit who is from God, so that we may understand what God has freely given us. This is what we speak, not in words taught us by human wisdom but in words taught by the Spirit, explaining spiritual realities with Spirit-taught words.

The person without the Spirit does not accept the things that come from the Spirit of God but considers them foolishness, and cannot

*understand them because they are discerned
only through the Spirit. The person with the
Spirit makes judgments about all things,
but such a person is not subject to merely
human judgments, for, "Who has known
the mind of the Lord so as to instruct him?"
But we have the mind of Christ.*

This clarifies the role of the Holy Spirit in the life of a
believer. He indoctrinates us and teaches us God's truth,
and will make sure that we are not surrendering to the system of this world or the world's way of doing things. He
will make sure that we are following the truth as it is laid
out for us in the word of God. "But when He, the Spirit of
truth, comes, He will guide you into all the truth. He will
not speak on His own; He will speak only what He hears,
and He will tell you what is yet to come," Jesus says in John
16:13. The Holy Spirit helps us to understand the true pathway to righteousness (right standing with God).

The Holy Spirit also communicates the will of God to
us and helps us communicate with God. Through the communication of God's will by the Holy Spirit flow the blessings that God has for us. In Romans 8:26 the Bible states,
"In the same way, the Spirit helps us in our weakness. We

do not know what we ought to pray for, but the Spirit Himself intercedes for us through wordless groans."The Holy Spirit prays and hits the target for us. He actually captures our prayer and makes sure that God receives it after we have prayed. Our faith (the belief that God will do what we have asked Him to do) precedes the understanding, but we need the Holy Spirit for that understanding. He causes us to transcend our current situation and be endowed with God's power to achieve our God-given purpose here on earth.

The Holy Spirit also bears witness to our kingdom ambassadorship. He verifies our authenticity as children of the Most High God. Therefore, as God's children, we should ask Him for everything, even the power to walk in the fullness of our calling. When Jesus came to the Jews, they were expecting a king that fit their definition, definitely not someone who was born in a manger and worked as a carpenter. Know that your calling may not fit man's definition or be of his understanding. In fact, it shouldn't, because man did not call you—God did. That's why it's imperative that you walk in obedience by the Holy Spirit. When your steps are ordered by God, then you are blessed.

Let me share a personal story to illustrate this.

My first experience outside of the classroom as an assistant principal happened in a district that was histori-

cally segregated. (God has used me several times in my life to be the first in breaking the color barrier on multiple educational fronts.) At this particular school, I was prepped for what to expect in a lunch conversation with my new principal. He let me know what his cultural beliefs were about African Americans and the amount of support I could expect from him as a result.

I began to pray about this assignment and soon recognized God's hand in it. I found the courage to accept the assignment, and searched consistently for my purpose there. When I initially showed up for work, I let my peers and staff know that I was a practicing Christian, and that that was the center of my leadership style. It set the precedence for everything I did from that moment on for that school.

I was one of two assistant principals in a middle school environment. The school had a serious gang problem, which we battled daily. One day I was in the cafeteria, and a student threatened me by clasping his hands together and pointing his fingers at me as if he was firing a gun. He was expelled eventually; however, he returned to school under false pretense to return his books and other school property as required. He brought two of his gang members with him.

I was called to the front office in the absence of the building principal because these young men were disturbing the office staff. I escorted them out to the hallway, and they began to joke with me. One young man stuck his hands in his pockets, and when I asked what was in his pocket, he refused to identify the object and spoke something in Spanish to the other two students. One of them distracted me while the young man pulled out his gun. He was so nervous that he dropped it, and I reminded them all I could have them arrested for having a gun on school property. To my surprise, the gang member picked up the gun and ran out of the school with no incident. I later thought, "They have the gun, and are running away from me!" They were arrested later that day.

I share this story to show that, because I was operating in my God-purpose, I was protected from the imminent harm that the gang members could have inflicted on me. Instead, because of my position in Christ, no harm came my way that day, nor was anyone else harmed as a result of the malicious intent of those young men.

An incident with that young man later occurred, in a local park where he shot and killed another gang member. He was arrested, tried, and eventually served prison time.

HOW DO I *BE* THE SPIRITUAL ME?

Every person has a specific gift or talent from God. Sometimes there is more than one talent given to an individual. What are you good at doing? What do you have a passion for? What goals or thoughts about *becoming* keep you up late at night or wake you up early in the morning? What is it that people say you are good at? What dreams and visions have you had regarding your future?

Proverbs 22:29 talks about the God kind of success. "Do you see someone skilled in their work? They will serve before kings; they will not serve before officials of low rank." It is your spiritual mission to find out what constitutes God-success for your life.

Who will be blessed by your gifts and talents? Remember, blessing people with your gifts inspires them to fulfill their calling. The God-kind of **SUCCESS** can be remembered as:

Success
Ultimately
Comes with
Consistent
Efforts and
Simply
Stated...**GOALS** (**G**odly **O**rdained **A**chievement
Leaves **S**atisfaction)

Now that's deep!

Goals have deadlines. Dreams do not. All things work together for your good when you walk in your purpose and become who God has called you to be.

How do you get there? You do so with prayer every step along the way.

Praying is a two-way conversation with God. Sure, you can ask in His name and receive; however, you must listen and recognize God's voice and the answer He gives you. Sometimes the answer is "Yes," other times it is "No," and finally it could be "Wait."

Always ask God for wisdom in every aspect of your life. Ask for patience to wait on His response. God does not require things to change overnight. Sacrificing the desire for an immediate answer involves denying our flesh; diligence is often required. You must take on the attitude that, "If it is to be, it is up to me with God's help." Be determined to see this to the end and do not give up. Do not let anything stop you from pursuing and walking in your purpose. Developing your faith with these characteristics will keep you energized until you see the full manifestation of your calling.

You cannot be measured by the world's standards. Successfully pursue and attain total peace and fulfillment

in every aspect of your life. With the Holy Spirit's help, you can do it! Therefore, be true to your purpose and commit to walking in your purpose with excellence.

Everything that God does is the definition of *good*. As a matter of fact, Jesus said in Matthew 19:17 that"…there is none good but one, that is, God."When we compare God's good to our good, we are bankrupt. Our "good enough" is the enemy of excellence. When we operate with a servant's heart, we walk as servants, not status seekers.

God's purpose requires us to be willing to count the cost. The size or status of a person's reputation is based on the obstacle it takes to stop them from fulfilling their purpose. There are some things that God wants to do for you that your friends will not be a part of, which will impact your circle of influence or your membership in the "Me Too Club. Show me your friends, and I will show you your future.

Your purposeful foundation is rooted in *love*. Love God, love others, and love yourself. Love God enough to fulfill His purpose for your life. Love others enough to lead them to Christ, but don't allow them to deter you from achieving your purpose. Love yourself enough to be willing to go on the journey and receive all that God has for you within this purpose-driven life.

Know the season that you are in; preparing and sowing for God's purpose is serious business. Make accomplishing the necessary tasks a priority. Do not be afraid to step out of the boat like the apostle Peter into uncharted territory. Take authority over any negative thoughts or outside negative influences. Do not let other people take away your liberty to fulfill your purpose in Jesus Christ. If you are experiencing trouble in that area, fast and pray the Scriptural word for a renewed mind. Then, guard your spiritual health by reading and meditating on God's words found in the Bible. (Self-help books will not achieve what the Word of God does. The Holy Spirit is always available to assist you in understanding what the Word is saying to you.)

Go after Jesus and His purpose with all that you have! Develop an expectation for a "purpose-filled expected end." It is worth the wait. Assuming a posture of waiting will:

1. Get you more than you expected;
2. Keep you covered securely under the wings of God's protection;
3. Get you that heavenly answer from God in *His* perfect timing, because you are called by Him.

God begins with the appointment before He actually interviews you for the job, because He knows He can equip you for it. He examines your internal fiber rather than your outward adornment. In this process, He will strengthen you so that you are guaranteed to win. However, you must show up for the interview. Again I say, "Wait on the Lord!"

HOW DO WE HEAR FROM GOD?

Location, location, location! Getting into the right spiritual location is a key element to hearing from God. It must be noise free, and you must be physically and mentally aligned. The proverbial spiritual statement is, "Speak, Lord, for your servant is listening" (see 1 Samuel 3:1–10). Listen for a still, small voice. Sometimes we miss the small things because of the major distractions in and around us. Get quiet. Ask God for forgiveness to clear the spiritual airwaves. Confess that you are not patient, if that is the case. Be still, sit down, and *be quiet*. God will get your attention by any means necessary.

Habakkuk 2:2–3 lays the foundation for hearing from God. It says:

> *Then the Lord replied, "Write down the revelation and make it plain on tablets so that*

> *a herald may run with it. For the revelation*
> *awaits an appointed time; it speaks of the*
> *end and will not prove false. Though it linger,*
> *wait for it; it will certainly come and will not*
> *delay."*

Tarry awhile. We must spend time worshipping God in Spirit and in truth.

Getting in the spiritual location with God can be hard work for some people. However, it is necessary. Again, if you are not patient, then acknowledge that to God. Eventually, you will cultivate the art of listening, meditating, and praying the Scriptures.

Seek God in every circumstance. Seek to connect the dots regarding your life and your present circumstances to understand how God is moving you to your "purposed-filled destiny." Flow in the anointing He has on your life, being led by the Holy Spirit.

As hope goes, so does your faith. Faith without works is dead. Our world is shaped by the words we utter. Watch your words. Keep growing in the things of God and speak aloud what you are expecting. Do not give up. Do not fear. Fear says that what you see on the outside is greater than what you believe on the inside. Fear also says that you do not trust God. Stand on your spiritual foundation.

It is important that you do something great for God, including believing you can have what you pray for. It is certainly not over until you win! Remember to acknowledge that you were created by the Supreme Being, God who is the Winner, the Victorious One. Believe in the Winner with your whole heart, mind, and strength. Celebrate your victories along the way privately and publicly so that God gets the glory.

HOW DO I *BE* ME IN A CHURCH SETTING?

Ecclesiastes 5:1–2 sets spiritual precedence for church protocol. It states:

Guard your steps when you go to the house of God. Go near to listen rather than to offer the sacrifice of fools, who do not know that they do wrong. Do not be quick with your mouth, do not be hasty in your heart to utter anything before God. God is in heaven and you are on earth, so let your words be few.

There is right and wrong behavior everywhere in our society. The house of God is no different. Doing what is right in a church setting according to God's Holy Word requires you to study His Word. Then you will be able to prosper in the wisdom of God; others will too, having been associated with you.

You will never rise above the limitations of your character. The level of your character will determine your levels of anointing and prosperity in the body of Christ. Conquer the real enemy in "me." You do that by:

1. Identifying your unspiritual behavior (see Ephesians 5:17–21)
2. Changing your unspiritual behavior (stop making excuses)
3. Committing to the change until the change is evident

Once you work on your character, embracing God's call for your life and being all God has called you to be is the next step. When you are living according to His purpose, being and doing what God has called you to is your highest gift to Him.

PRAYER TO BE ALL THAT GOD HAS CALLED YOU TO BE

You are great and greatly to be praised. Elohim, You are all powerful and wise. Faithful and righteous You are to me. Let Your will be done in my life as I worship You in spirit and in truth. Give me the strength each day to be all that You want me to be as I embrace all that You have destined for my life. Help me to live a life of purpose. Please forgive me for not pursuing your purpose as first priority in my life. Deliver me from the evil influences that prohibit me from doing so, and equip me for Your kingdom purpose so that I may glorify You in all that I do. It is my heart's desire to please You and only You.

Forever and ever, In the Name of Jesus, Amen.

Chapter Three Questions :

TO BE OR NOT TO BE

1. How will you as a believer *be* a Christian?
2. How will you a believer be more like Christ?
3. What steps will you as a believer take to "draw nigh to God"?
4. What role will the Holy Spirit play in your life to become more like Christ?
5. How will God use His servant to help you *be* all that He has called you to be?

CHAPTER 4

Praying for Discernment and Listening Ears

*"So I say to you: Ask and it will be given to you;
seek and you will find; knock and the door will be
opened to you." (Luke 11:9)*

Conversing with God has always been a key component in my spiritual walk, so it was not unusual that one night, I just sat quietly and listened to God speak to me. As He spoke I began to write down exactly what I heard Him say:

"Do not forsake your first love, Jesus Christ, and My relationship with you. Do not be afraid of what you are about to suffer. Be faithful, even to the point of death, and I will give you the crown of life. He who

*has an ear, let him hear what the Spirit
says to the body of Christ. He who over-
comes will not be hurt at all by the second
death. You remain true to My name, My faithful witness; however, repent. He who has an
ear let him hear."*

My response was, "Thank you, Father, for good health,
beauty, gentleness, kindness, longsuffering, joy, and peace.
You have truly, wonderfully, and marvelously blessed me,
and I am so thankful. I will not abuse my body nor allow
anyone to abuse me. My heart is fixed, and I am more alert
than ever before. Give me Your desires for me, and I will
pay attention and listen."

He said, "Be watchful and strengthen the things that
remain, for I have not found thy works perfect. Always
have a kind word, as well as doing a kind deed in regards
to others. Continue with Bible study. Draw nearer to Mrs.
Allen. Draw nearer to Lily." (These are individuals who have
been Christian role models to me.)

I wrote back, "Thank You for sending help to me with
the store. (I previously owned a quaint boutique and required some assistance in the overall management of the
store). The entire team has their unique gifts and talents

for the store. Thank You for my husband, Gene. You have elevated his mind and increased his desire to support me. Keep him close to You and focused on being a wonderful husband. You have brought our circumstances under your sovereign decree.

"I pray in the Name of God Almighty, the Father and Jesus Christ, for the protection of the United States of America, our community, and our leaders. God you govern and are over all!"

What a wonderful conversation with God.... I am so glad I captured it on paper.

Sometimes God speaks to you in a still small voice, through other Christians, through the Bible, or through prayer. In this chapter we will be discussing how to seek God in prayer for discernment.

The word discernment is defined on Dictionary.com as "the faculty of discerning; discrimination; acuteness of judgment and understanding." Discerning means to simply recognize, identify, or diagnose something. As believers, we must ask God for spiritual discernment or insight into His will or way for our lives in order to fulfill our purpose.

The Holy Spirit is the vehicle that communicates to us and through us to God. He is our divine interpreter. Yet,

we also have to be ready for the communication to take place, and there are some things that we need to do prior to being able to discern God's voice.

You must first ask God to give you listening ears and to teach you how to know His voice so that you are not listening to a voice that may sound something like His. 2 Corinthians 11:14b states, "...for Satan himself masquerades as an angel of light." In Matthew 4, there is a very interesting conversation between Jesus and Satan. Satan tries to use the Word of God to entrap Jesus. If he tried to tempt Jesus with the Word of God, he will most definitely try to confuse you by imitating God's voice!

In an article in the popular devotional *Our Daily Bread*, entitled "Call to Me, "Satan's method of communication were identified by the following indicators:

- **Tone:** accusing, nagging, and mocking. Generates fear and causes confusion.
- **Vague:** generates an overall sense of guilt, as if everything is wrong. Creates feeling of hopelessness and weakness.
- **Discouraging:** attacks your self-confidence, tells you that you are weak and worthless.
- **Brings up the past:** replays your sin and shame, reminds you of your poor choices.

- **Rejecting:** produces the feeling that God has rejected you as unworthy and unholy. Portrays God as judge and you as a miserable sinner.
- **Isolating:** gives suggestions that cause you to withdraw from others.
- **Negative:** tells you that the horrible way you feel is [just] the way it is.

We become familiar with God's voice as we build a relationship with Him. Remember that the Holy Spirit is the conduit for our conversation with God. The article goes on to say that when God is speaking to us, the Holy Spirit's communication is different:

- **Tone:** gentle, loving, imploring, and urges your return to Him.
- **Specific:** tells you to take a specific action in response to sin; freedom follows.
- **Encouraging:** says you can rely on His power, not your strength.
- **Releases you from the past:** tells you your sins are forgiven, never to be held against you.
- **Attracts:** generates an expectation of kindness, love, and a new beginning with His help.

- **Draws into fellowship:** sends others to minister to you in love, as well as sends you to others. Speaks of His unchanging nature and steadfast love.
- **Truthful:** states the facts about you and God.

In an earlier chapter, we discussed the necessity of getting into a quiet place in a remote location and getting in a position to listen for the voice of God. When you conduct a two-way conversation with someone, it's critical that the environment around you is clear of all distractions, that you are comfortable and prepared, with pen and paper if necessary, to hear from God. You want to show up for your time with God with an acute physical and mental awareness. You have asked for His presence, so bring an expectancy of hearing from Him because you are God's servant.

Hearing from God is a spiritual privilege. When you extend an invitation to Him to join you in a conversation, His response is a gift.

A good way to get an extensive understanding of how to hear God's voice is to actually study the art of listening. In our extremely busy society, we sometimes lose the skill that we so readily take for granted. The Bible compels us to "study to show ourselves approved" by God. He often

shows up in a still quiet voice but unfortunately sometimes we miss that because we are looking for a particular kind of sign or word from God.

Patience is another key to hearing from God. He is not necessarily on our timetable. Sometimes we must "tarry," as the old saints use to say, lingering in our prayer closet, singing praises to His holy name, until He arrives.

Additionally, praise and worship is an important preliminary position to get in tune with God. The Psalmist David said in Psalm 22:3, "But thou art holy, O thou that inhabitest the praises of Israel." According to this Scripture, God can't help but show up when we are offering Him the sacrifice of praise.

Asking God for forgiveness is also a valuable factor in hearing God's voice. We should not only ask for forgiveness of our sins, but also seek forgiveness from those that we have sinned against. Colossians 3:12–13 states,

> *Therefore, as God's chosen people, holy and dearly loved, clothe yourselves with compassion, kindness, humility, gentleness and patience. Bear with each other and forgive one another if any of you has a grievance against someone. Forgive as the Lord forgave you. And over all these virtues*

put on love, which binds them all together in perfect unity.

It pleases the heart of God when we are in unity with our fellow brethren; resentfulness on the other hand, will hinder your ability to hear from God.

God also speaks to us through His prophets. In the Old and New Testament, there is evidence of God's prophets changing the face of the nations of Israel and Judah through their prophetic utterances. God also uses modern-day prophets to speak to His people, nations, and the world. As it says in 2 Peter 1:19–21:

> *We also have the prophetic message as something completely reliable, and you will do well to pay attention to it, as to a light shining in a dark place, until the day dawns and the morning star rises in your hearts. Above all, you must understand that no prophecy of Scripture came about by the prophet's own interpretation of things. For prophecy never had its origin in the human will, but prophets, though human, spoke from God as they were inspired by the Holy Spirit.*

Meditation is also a good prepping tool for hearing God's voice. Pondering on His word and memorizing Scripture feeds your spirit and strengthens your spiritual muscles. God has given you His Word as an authenticating tool for anything you may hear in regards to His purpose for your life. He desires more than anything to be able to commune with you. That's why He sent Jesus Christ, His only begotten Son, to die for your sins. God wanted nothing to stand in the way of His communicating with you; therefore, you must make it a priority to not allow anything to stand in the way of your communicating with Him. (Selah!)

PRAYER FOR DISCERNMENT

Adonai, the possessor of my life, You are the one who gives gifts and equips me for Your divine purpose. I am not my own, because I have been bought with a price, the precious blood of the Lamb! My spirit, soul, and body belong to You. I trust You and You only to speak to me and give me the discernment that allows me to hear Your voice and intimately know Your will for my life. Let Your will be done, let Your kingdom come in the name of Jesus, on this day and in the days to come. Forgive me for allowing the busyness of my life to interfere with our communication. I decree

and declare that I know the voice of the Good Shepherd and the voice of a stranger which I will not follow.

Exalted King, Emmanuel, there is no other god like You. You are great and Your name is greatly to be praised. May I know undeniably in my heart of hearts Your will, and submit to it readily with an obedient and willing spirit. Give me ears to hear Your voice, and may the Holy Spirit be my constant companion as I willingly pursue my purpose for the honor of Your kingdom's sake.

In the Name of Jesus, Amen and praise the Lord!

Chapter Four Questions:

PRAYING FOR DISCERNMENT

1. How will you hear what God is saying to you?
2. How will you know that it is God and not yourself or the devil talking to you?
3. What is praying for discernment, and how will it fit into your Christian walk?
4. When should you pray for discernment?
5. Is it okay to ask God for a sign if you are not sure it is Him you are hearing?

CHAPTER 5

Life Happens...

"Then the Lord replied, 'Write down the revelation and make it plain on tablets so that a herald may run with it.'" (Habakkuk 2:2)

Simply speaking, when "life happens," you handle the trials and tribulations that come your way by trusting God. He has promised to never leave you or forsake you. Once you establish a relationship with Him, you get to understand His nature and personality. You begin to understand that your trials and tribulations will make you stronger and that you will be victorious in the end.

It is sometimes hard for some people to imagine these results, especially when they are going through those trials. The operative words in that sentence, though, are "going through"; you are not going to stay in those trials.

Having God as a partner in this trial dictates that you will be victorious, because He always has the last word. The proper posture to assume is trust in God and belief that the situation is not permanent. Everything must change! As you walk through those changes, you will see that God is there for you.

The next thing that is of vital importance when life happens is that you must praise your way through the circumstance. Lift up your hands and praise God simply because He is worthy to be praised. Earlier we mentioned how God "inhabits the praises of His people." If you want to feel the presence of God in the middle of a battle, start praising Him. The Lord had His people praise Him before the wall of Jericho came tumbling down and He showed up in a mighty way; Joshua and the mighty men of God were able to take the city as a result. Praise will get you through any circumstance or trial; you've got to believe that. It's hard for some people to believe, and it's hard for some people to even do, but you've got to be able to say, whatever the trial is, "Lord, I believe and trust You. I will praise You in the good times and the bad."

Thanking God for the wisdom and fortitude to endure the trial is also key when posturing yourself to stay on course in pursuing your purpose. It is an instrument used

by you to ensure the God-outcome. There are others who will be blessed by your testimony (defined by Dictionary. com as an "open declaration or profession, as of faith"). Hebrews 11:1 says, "Now faith is the substance of things hoped for, the evidence of things not seen." The blessing in a trial is generally the testimony that you have.

God does not bring trials or tribulations in your life; they are there as part of the whole lifecycle. God is, how-ever, standing by you every step of the way. He will make sure that everything happens for your good. Even in trials and tribulations, you've got to have stamina, be persistent and steadfast, hold on, have tenacity, and be determined that you are not going to give up. Ultimately, it's between you and God in terms of getting through and getting the victory.

I say all of this because sometimes these trials carry long-suffering with them. You must suffer with dignity, not succumbing to the negative voices that are telling you that you can't make it. If you have someone here on earth that you trust, share your experience with them. No one has to go through trials or tribulations alone while here on earth. That's why God sends us the Holy Spirit, who will allow you to discern who to call and who to allow

into your close circle to help walk you through the trial or tribulation.

While I was going about my day as a boutique owner, one of the ladies from the church came by and delivered a Sketch Pad book, sent to me by Mrs. Jean Hines Caldwell (better known as Mom Caldwell). Mom Caldwell was noted for her wisdom and desire to share with younger women in an effort to lead them into a "better state of life." The lady that delivered the Sketch Pad commented, "I don't know why she would send you this." Inside the cover of the Sketch Pad, though, were these words: "Jackie, when you feel stress, sketch! Whatever. It helps! The title of your shop and the arrangements prove you have imagination. So use it!"

Here is what I realized: Life happens. The sicknesses and diseases of love ones happened, like the prolonged illness and death of my mother and husband, two people whom I loved so much. Physical and mental pain happened, which I experienced as a result of a terrible automobile accident, coupled with the recovery and therapy process that challenged my mental capacity to handle the pain. My disobedience happened, when I spent more time on work and other folks' projects instead of answering God's call to complete this book. Life happens. Con-

sequently, I believe that each thing we do in life gives us experience for the next thing we will have an opportunity to do, and that our thoughtful planning is perfected by God when we place our trust in Him.

Mom Caldwell's note made me think. How could I use my keen imagination I used to create projects in the past which fostered some of my greatest achievements? How could I apply this same imagination to the difficult times, when "life" was happening *now*? How can you with your unique talents and circumstances?

The answer is to change your mind and release the difficulties to God. Change what you are thinking about (the problem) and how you are thinking (your attitude). Imagine differently and sketch that thing out. Use the SMART formula to create a **S**pecific, **M**easurable, **A**ttainable, **R**ealistic, and **T**ime-oriented plan instead of worrying or stressing about the trial.

James Allen, a British philosopher who lived around the turn of the twentieth century, stated, "All that a man achieves and all that he fails to achieve is the direct result of his own thoughts." When God changes your mind and your heart, you can run and not faint. Our thoughtful planning affects our self-image, our relationships, our health (physical, emotional, and spiritual), our priorities, the way

we manage our time, and our ability to enjoy life. God's plan for all of us is better than we can ever imagine. The best approach is to say, "God I trust you. You know what is best for me. Speak to my heart."

Know that He is on the throne. Do not hold on to your dream so tightly that God cannot get you to release it. Ask God to allow His will to be done, not yours, and release your dream so that it can go forth.

When we prove to God that we trust Him, then He will give us the desires of our heart Psalm 37:4 states, "Take delight in the LORD, and he will give you the desires of your heart." In order to walk with Him and release control, allowing things to fall in place, we must learn to trust Him.

Romans 12:2 says, "Be joyful in hope, patient in affliction, faithful in prayer. "When you have done all that you can, then wait on God. God will make things happen that you can never make happen for yourself. Do not live upset or frustrated. You can plant the prayer seed and water it, but only God will bring it to maturity.

Cast your cares on Him—worry ties the hand of God. Release control by having the attitude, "God, my life is in your hand." Take the pressure off yourself; you can't make a dream come true, and you can't heal yourself. Do your part, which is your responsibility, then trust God to do the rest in His timing.

God has you in the palm of His hand. Nothing happens unless He allows it to happen. Write your vision, sketch it out, release it to God, handle your own responsibility, keep a good attitude, and watch God change things! As Paul said, "Do not be anxious about anything, but in every situation, by prayer and petition, with thanksgiving, present your requests to God" (Philippians 4:6).

Remember to prioritize fulfilling your purpose in the middle of everything you are going through while "life happens."Knowing what your purpose is and staying connected to it daily is important. God gave us five senses, one of the strongest of which sight. Having a visual prioritization in the form of a vision board, scrapbook, or journal will act as a pictorial reminder of where you are headed, remembering Habakkuk 2:2: "Write down the revelation and make it plain on tablets so that a herald may run with it."God has instructed us to "write down"our vision so that we won't forget our destination.

It's good to revisit the vision to determine if we have moved away from His purpose. I also write notes in my Bible to memorialize my God-request, or a prophetic or revelatory word that I got from listening to a sermon or while in prayer. I use that as a checkpoint when I feel that

I might be straying in another direction and to keep my hope alive.

Prayer is also a major key factor during that period in life when things happen. Your mandate to fulfill God's purpose does not change, even though circumstances will change. Prayer acts as a rudder, and keeps us steadfastly moving forward on the route toward our destination. It strengthens us and encourages us to win the battle that we're fighting, but it also takes us to the next place in our purpose fulfilling journey.

I used the imagination Mom Caldwell reminded me that I had…and now, here I am, having survived the death of my loved ones, a crippling car accident, and writing this book. Yes, I dream big because I serve a God who delivers "big," heals "big," and will give me the desires of my heart. Allow my testimony to be an example for you, the miracle I have become and the "no worrying woman" I am now striving to be.

All things work together for the good.

A PRAYER FOR WHEN "LIFE HAPPENS"

Jehovah Nissi, my banner, You are the one who delivers and saves me when life happens. You give me victory. I thank You for the gift of life and life more abundantly.

Righteous Father, You are so patient for my sake, and You will not allow me to perish in the middle of life's changes. You will make sure that everything happens for my good. Thank You for the Holy Spirit. Forgive me for not consistently co-operating with You. Help me to learn the lessons from the trials.

Holy Spirit, show me the individuals that You have called alongside me in my circle of influence who I can share my cares and concerns with. Send me the prayer partner that you have ordained to walk beside me as I go through the trials and trib-ulations of life.

Compassionate Father, forgive me for allow-ing the cares of this world and the sins that so easily beset me to hold me captive to a life that is not pleasing to You. Please forgive me for not

always obeying Your Word. Forgive me for not wearing Your beautiful tapestry of glory for the good of others who are going through life challenges as well.

Jehovah Shalom, my God of peace, You give me divine rest in the middle of it all. Jesus, the Prince of Peace, lives in me. For His glory, In the Name of Jesus, Amen.

Chapter Five Questions:

LIFE HAPPENS...

1. When you are pursuing your purpose, how will you handle the trials and tribulations that come your way?

2. When life happens, how should you prioritize the things that affect you fulfilling your purpose?

3. How will you handle the conflicts with others who don't understand your purpose?

4. How will you handle the heartbreak of your purpose if it is not being endorsed by church leadership?

5. How will you deal with the negative voices within that prohibit you from fulfilling your purpose?

CHAPTER 6

Being Purpose Focused

*"The Lord will perfect that which concerneth me:
thy mercy, O Lord, endureth forever: forsake not
the works of thine own hands." (Psalm 138:8)*

When we are assured that we are walking on the pathway of God's purpose for our lives, we can count on Him to bless our good works. Being purpose focused means always having God's divine intent in mind and deliberately aligning everything in our lives around accomplishing that mandate.

When you are purpose focused, you have an intended future and plan for your life created by God. You've got to get in the center of that plan and His will for your life. You must know that your purpose and your future are

larger than anything else you can see, and that all is in the hands of God.

The Bible is full of examples of women and men who stayed purpose focused. We will discuss a few in this chapter.

Mary, the mother of Jesus, is our first example. When she was approached by the angel Gabriel with the news that she would be pregnant with the Messiah, she readily accepted the will of God for her life. "I am the Lord's servant," Mary answered. "May your word to me be fulfilled."(Luke 1:38) Remember that Mary was impregnated by the Holy Spirit during a time when women were stoned for much less than being pregnant out of wedlock. She was in her middle teens, too, and I'm sure her parents were puzzled about how something like this could happen to their daughter. She also had to explain her mysterious condition to her betrothed, Joseph. He knew that he had not been with Mary, but rather than her be publicly shamed, he sought to "put her away privately."Mary had to stand on her conviction to serve God amid much persecution. It's amazing when we consider the young girls of our time who are somewhere around Mary's age and how they would have handled a situation like this. Mary was committed and purposefully focused on God's mis-

sion for her life, which was to bear the Christ Child who had come to save the entire world. Mary is a prime example of how we should walk through a purpose focused life.

Let's take a look at another set of women who were purpose focused: Naomi and Ruth. Naomi, in the middle of her grief after losing her husband and both sons, decided to return to her hometown, Bethlehem. She implored her two daughters-in-law to return to their parents in Moab. Ruth decided to travel with Naomi as she returned to her homeland instead of returning to her parents' home. It was obvious to everyone around her that Ruth loved Naomi and dutifully cared for her needs. Ruth found herself in the harvesting field of Boaz, a kinsmen-redeemer of Naomi's. As soon as Naomi heard of the good fortune of Ruth, she began to devise a plan, coaching her daughter-in-law on the customs of that day and advising her how to posture herself for a kingdom blessing.

Naomi's purpose was to restore her household and find a husband for her daughter-in-law who had missed the opportunity of bearing a child when she was married to Naomi's son. Naomi took off her grieving clothes and sour continence when she began to see the revival that God had in store for her. She was reminded of her purpose and became tenacious in fulfilling the will of God for not

only her life but for that of her beloved daughter-in-law. As a result she got to help raise her grandchild Obed, King David's grandfather. Around the well, Naomi's good fortune was reported by the town's women:

> *The women said to Naomi: "Praise be to the Lord, who this day has not left you without a guardian-redeemer. May he become famous throughout Israel! He will renew your life and sustain you in your old age. For your daughter-in-law, who loves you and who is better to you than seven sons, has given him birth.*

Naomi was purpose focused, and God blessed her with her heart's desire.

Hannah is another example of a woman who was purpose focused. She was barren, wanted a child so badly that she told God if He gave her a child, she would give that child back to Him. So many women today are focused on their wish to have a child instead of focusing on the God who can make it happen for them. Pursuing God and His purpose requires that we put Him first in all that we do. Remember Matthew 6:33 that says, "But seek (aim for and strive after) first His kingdom and His righteousness (God's way of doing and being right), and then all

these things will be given to you as well" (AMP). All your needs will be met; everything else will fall into place. When you have a joyful expectation, something good can happen to you and through you. When you partner with God, you are headed toward your miracle. Hannah sought God, and He answered her prayer with a son named Samuel, who became one of the leading prophets in the Old Testament.

Our last biblical example of being purpose focused is King David. David learned how to love and trust God while he was shepherding sheep. Little did David know that his destiny included being king of all Israel, but he was faithful in the small things, so God could elevate him to the highest position in the land.

Yet, David was human and possessed a sin-nature like all of us. On many occasions he missed the mark of his high calling as king. He was a liar, murderer, and adulterer—to name a few of his faults!—but because of his repentant heart and love for God, he could remain purpose focused for God.

Sometimes you may get wrapped up in the notion that you are not good enough for Christ, but all you need is a repentant heart, as well as a broken and contrite spirit, and

God can do what is conceivably impossible for you in your life, simply because nothing is impossible for God.

David got the word that he would be king from the prophet Samuel fifteen years before he was actually crowned king of Judah. During that time, he was exiled from his home, hunted down by a madman, lived in caves, and fought many horrific battles. Yet David's unwavering love for God propelled him to remain purpose focused through it all, and he was a worshipper, writing many psalms to the Lord, expressing his love and faith in an unchangeable God.

All of these purpose focused biblical characters share a tenacity that is much needed in the body of Christ today.

Remember that the opposite of being purpose focused is being scatterbrained. Dictionary.com defines a scatterbrained person as "a person incapable of serious, connected thought." Surely that does not define you or the pursuit of your purpose! When you wake up in the morning rejoicing and being glad that you've been given another opportunity to serve God and achieve His purpose for your life, you are energized to be steadfast in your pursuit of it. If you get up in the morning with a to-do list for God that is filled with things that will positively impact someone's life and yours, you are destined to win. Be intention-

al about what you are doing for God every day, regardless of what life brings your way, because this sets you up for a prosperous day. At the end of the day, you have the benefit of coming back and checking those things off with great satisfaction in your accomplished mission. Refrain from going through the day trying to make things happen, and then getting frustrated when they don't because you were doing them in your own strength. I believe that the quality of your life improves drastically when you make pleasing God your objective.

As I mentioned earlier, my mother purposed for me to be an educator/academic leader and to help children. In my youth I was constantly given opportunities to grow in those areas at home, church, and in the community. There was a brief time when the pursuit of a secular singing career was premiere in my life. However, God orchestrated my pathway to the purpose that He predestined for me to walk in as an educator. Once I was assured that I was on God's pathway, I have not strayed from my purpose.

We all experience distractions that try to pull us in another direction, as was the case when I wanted to sing instead of teach. Satan is an expert at getting you enthralled in things that are not relevant to your purpose—this may cause you to be derailed. He will use insecurity as a tac-

tic. He will use other people as a tactic. Jesus experienced this with Peter, when they were discussing who He was. Out of all the disciples, Peter was the one who said that Jesus was the "Messiah, the Son of the Living God." Soon after Jesus told the disciples that He would be facing His imminent death in Jerusalem, Peter rebuked Jesus; then Jesus rebuked him:: "Jesus turned and said to Peter, 'Get behind me, Satan! You are a stumbling block to me; you do not have in mind the concerns of God, but merely human concerns'" (Matthew 16:23).

If you ever find yourself derailed, getting back on track is simple. Remind yourself of what your purpose is in life. Ask God for direction through prayer, and expect Him to put you back on the pathway to living a purpose focused life.

PRAYER FOR
BEING PURPOSE FOCUSED

Triumphant Father, I thank You for Your direction and the knowledge of the path You are leading me to travel. Thank You for reminding me of my God-ordained purpose and the unique mission for my life.

Help me to keep Your divine intent on my mind as I plan for the future. Keep me humble, approachable, and kind while experiencing every good thing You have for me. Direct me to bless others while encouraging them to bless their families and fellow church members. May thy kingdom become real in my life and in the lives of others that You have called me to, as I focus my attention on fulfilling Your divine purpose for my life.

May I put my hand to the plow and not look back on yesterday's sorrows or successes, but may I cherish the road that lies ahead that is full of God possibilities as I focus first and foremost on You and Your will being done. In the Name of Jesus, Amen.

Chapter Six Questions:

BEING PURPOSE FOCUSED

1. What does being purpose focused mean to you?
2. Give some biblical or present examples of men and women that you can relate to who remained purpose focused.
3. What is the opposite of being purpose focused?
4. What are some common tactics that the enemy uses to derail you from your purpose?
5. How will you get back on track (being purpose focused) after you've been temporarily derailed?

CHAPTER 7

The Purpose-Driven Sacrifice

"…but those who hope in the Lord will renew
their strength. They will soar on wings like eagles;
they will run and not grow weary, they will walk
and not be faint." (Isaiah 40:31)

Over two thousand years ago, on a desolate hilltop, a righteous man died unjustly. So many other men have died over the course of history, but this Man was different. He was the long-awaited Messiah.

His people had been waiting for Him for centuries. Many prophetic promises had been made about this King of Kings, and many hearts were filled with the anticipation of His arrival. Yet here He was, stretched out on a cross, dying a brutal death for all mankind. His people despised Him because He brought no pomp and circumstance to

His kingdom. He was a simple man, actually a carpenter like His earthly father, and the son of Mary, a poor Jewish girl.

It bewildered the mind of common men that this Man, who some said was a prophet, could be a king: there were moments when one was in His presence that they sensed the tangible hand of God working through Him. But others had come before Him claiming to be the Messiah and were found to be counterfeits. This Man, well…He was different. Contrary to the popular belief at the time, He was Jesus, the promised King of all Kings.

He was crucified because *someone* had to pay the price for the sins of all mankind. It was His purpose-driven sacrifice. What is yours? Take a moment and review Isaiah 53 before continuing.

There will be times in your life that God will ask you to make a "purpose-driven sacrifice," just like He asked His Son to do. Determine *now* what your response will be. If you accept the mission, God has promised to make you a joint-heir with His Son, who is seated at His right hand praying for you without cessation to complete your mission successfully, if you should decide to accept it.

WHAT IS A PURPOSE-DRIVEN SACRIFICE?

A purpose-driven sacrifice is one where God requires us to mirror a Christ-like response to the trials, tribulations, and accusations of others in our everyday life as we pursue His purpose. When we ask ourselves if this is possible for mortal man, we should take a look at Abraham.

God first revealed to Abraham that he would be the father of many nations when he called him to leave his country and go to the land God would show him. Abraham was seventy-five years old. Fifteen years later, when Abraham was ninety, God renewed his promise. Ten years later, at age one hundred, Abraham and Sarah finally had their son.[2]

Abraham and Sarah waited a long time to see the manifestation of God's promise in their lives! Then when Isaac was of age, God told Abraham to offer him up as a sacrifice in the land of Moriah! Abraham, in his obedience to God, reluctantly took his son to the mountaintop. As he was about to begin the ritual, the Angel of the Lord called to him to stop. It had been a test of Abraham's obedience. God allowed Abraham to go through this trial to demonstrate his total trust and dependence on Him.

---

2) www.explorefaith.org/time/fullness.html

In order for us to progressively pursue our purpose, we should be prepared to make a purpose-driven sacrifice.

Although God has not asked us to put our children on the altar, He has required us to make sacrifices in our lives, including changing bad behaviors or developing good ones in our lives in order to honor Him.

Forgiveness is one of those behaviors we must work out. We must first understand how important it is to forgive, and we must choose to forgive those who have trespassed against us. Similarly, we must practice forgetting those things from the past that keep us down. We have to forget those events in the past which have marred our lives and the sins that we have committed, in order to walk uprightly before God.

Modeling Christ's behavior is key to us progressing toward "the mark of our high calling."

There was a woman that the religious leaders of the day brought to Jesus, caught in the act of adultery. The punishment for adultery at that time was stoning. The beauty of the situation was Jesus' response. He knew that the leaders had come to trap Him into saying something contrary to the Mosaic Law. Yet in His infinite wisdom, He caused them to do an internal reflection on their own sin life when He said, "All right, but let the one who has never

sinned throw the first stone!" (John 8:7b NLT). The point was that there is no one on the face of the earth who has not sinned and fallen short of the mark of God's purpose for their lives…except for Jesus. He extends mercy to those He forgives, and expects *us* to do likewise.

Modeling Christ in His readiness to forgive, forget, and extend grace to others shows our appreciation for the grace that He has appropriated us, and honors His crucial sacrifice on the cross. God's grace is more powerful than any sin that we have committed. Sometimes, in our own strength, this may seem impossible, but in God all things are possible. Ultimately we have to give up the past and stop looking in the rearview mirror. God has us to move beyond our past, knowing that our purpose is not just for ourselves but also for others. We must live a certain way so that we ultimately draw others to Christ. This is our true purpose in life as a Christian.

God uses man and woman on earth to draw others to Him. God doesn't ask us to die an eternal death for Him, but He does ask us to live for Him.

THERE WAS "PEE" IN THE PAIN

This past year, I was in a horrific car accident. The miracle was that no one died as a result of the head-on collision.

One Sunday, driving home from church, my blood pressure hit an all-time low, and I blacked out at the wheel.

The accident resulted in severe injuries to my head, face, shoulder and lower extremities. In fact, the doctor told me that I was bleeding from my brain as well, and also needed cosmetic surgery for a fractured bone that was holding my eye in place. For a while, I was totally immobile and had to rely on the help of nursing staff to get around.

One night, I woke up with a keen urgency to urinate, but couldn't locate the nurses' call button because I was incoherent. I finally found it, but when I pressed the button for assistance, no one came. As I laid there in one of the most vulnerable positions a human being could be in, I was forced to pee right where I was. I attempted to cover myself with the pad that they had placed underneath me; I didn't have any control over what was happening to me, and wanted to maintain the little dignity that I had left. I knew eventually someone would come and find me in this state of disarray, and I was helpless to do anything about it.

God chose that time to visit me and share a crucial revelation. He said that in order to live a life of purpose, I must be willing to develop the fruit of *perseverance*.

Laying in that hospital bed, I could let this experience derail me permanently from God's plan for my life to prosper me and keep me in good health as my soul prospers. Instead, I chose to praise God, pray for myself and others, and listen for the voice of God. I also prayed, decreed, and declared that no weapon formed against me would prosper. I was going to fight (persevere) through my pain to live and not die. I also asked God to heal my head injuries and face. As a result of my perseverance through persistent praying and the love God showed me, no surgeries were necessary for my brain or face.

My expectancy was that God would continue to provide me with what I needed to complete His God-assignment on my life. Ultimately, I had to learn to walk again and use the hand, foot, and shoulder that were broken. Just like Abraham did not waver in His expectation that God would provide a lamb for his sacrifice when he and Isaac went to the mountain, I did not waver in my *expectation*. Instead, I looked for the expedient pathway back to fulfilling my God-purpose and expected God to heal me fully.

Lastly, I *exalted* my God and remained in the assurance that "this too will pass." In this revelation, I was able to receive my complete restoration and sing God's praises to everyone who visited me. My healing has been called

"miraculous," and my recovery was fast and in record time from such horrific injuries.

You may ask why I've chosen to be so transparent and share this story with you. Well, Christ wasn't embarrassed to go to the cross for sins He did not commit. He bravely faced utter destruction on Golgotha because of them. He bore it all for me, and I choose to bare it all for Him. It was impossible to survive that car accident without God's grace and mercy covering me.

There isn't one iota of our lives that God won't use to exalt His kingdom, if we allow Him to do so. God took my PEE in my pain revelation and turned it into something that is going to bless everyone who reads this book. His purpose is to take every area of our lives and use it for His glory. When facing a purpose-driven sacrifice, remember that assuming a posture of PEE (perseverance, expectation, and exaltation) will empower you to successfully move forward as you successfully move forward as you are called *According to His Purpose*.

PRAYER FOR MASTERING
THE PURPOSE-DRIVEN SACRIFICE

Heavenly Father, thank You for the ultimate sacrifice, Jesus Christ, who died for my sins and the sins of the whole wide world. Because of His purpose-driven sacrifice, I can become a joint-heir with your Son, who is seated at Your victorious right hand praying for me.

Thank You, Lord, for allowing me to better understand that perseverance, expectation, and exaltation are necessary to live a sacrificial lifestyle for Your glory.

Almighty God! You are mighty, strong, and first in my purpose-driven life. You are all-sufficient and all-bountiful. You are the one who is more than enough. Thank You for taking care of me and meeting my every need in the midst of every trial and tribulation that I experience. For in You, all things work out for the good of those who are called According to Your Purpose.

In the Name of Jesus, Amen.

Chapter Seven Questions:

BEING PURPOSE-FOCUSED

1. What does being purpose-focused mean to you?
2. Give some biblical or present examples of men and women that you can relate to who remained purpose-focused
3. What is the opposite of being purpose-focused?
4. What are some common tactics that the enemy uses to derail you from your purpose?
5. How will you get back on track after you've been temporary derailed?

CHAPTER 8

Being in the World and Not of It

"Do not conform to the pattern of this world,
but be transformed by the renewing of your mind.
Then you will be able to test and approve what God's will
is—His good, pleasing, and perfect will." (Romans 12:2)

The world is a colossal stage which we get an opportunity to live out our lives upon. For a Christian, it is the place where we fulfill the Great Commission that Jesus left us at His ascension. In Matthew 28:18–20, here is the mandate He left for His followers:

> *All authority in heaven and on earth has been*
> *given to Me. Therefore go and make disciples*
> *of all nations, baptizing them in the name*
> *of the Father and of the Son and of the Holy*

> *Spirit, and teaching them to obey everything*
> *I have commanded you. And surely I am with*
> *you always, to the very end of the age.*

As we pursue our purpose, we must remember to use spiritual tools to accomplish our spiritual work on the earth.

Being a heavenly ambassador for the kingdom purpose means that we are a reflection of Christ on the earth. Christ rules the heavens and has appropriated us for dominion in the earth. He's the head ambassador for heaven, who came down to earth to show us how to live a kingdom-purposed life, thus encouraging us to strive to replicate the life of Christ, and act as His representatives of heaven here on earth.

Assuming the position of a Christian requires that we *be* like Christ. We do this so that His purpose can be manifested to draw others into the kingdom and to this Christian walk. In doing so, we must release those things that are not pleasing to God and those things that will prohibit a person from coming to Christ. Believing in God is great, and getting to heaven is great; however, fulfilling your God-given purpose on earth is instrumental to the overall kingdom mission in Matthew 28. Being Christ-

like requires us to walk on the same pathway that Jesus walked. The clarity in knowing what that walk should be and how it should be carried out is crucial to your Christian mandate.

The contrast to that is actually being in the world and not of the world. It is evident that we are in the Last Days. We see a rise in the amount of exposure to perversion, profanity, and immoral behavior in the airways and on television. We see a lot of abnormal behavior that appears to be normal because it is so pervasive. Back in my mother's day, the soap operas, like *The Young and The Restless* and *Days of Our Lives*, were not as nearly provocative and sexually driven as what we see on modern day television. Even the Internet has become a deadly trap for those who seek out pornography and sexual deviation. Everything has gotten terribly out of hand. People are stepping away from normal behavior and putting their personal pleasures above normal, respectable behavior, both Christian and non-Christians alike. This mode of behavior is registering as normal behavior in the minds of people who are not Christ-like.

What are we doing? We are creating a subculture that is built on abnormal behavior, especially for the present day Christian. Due to the prevalent, intrusive nature of

this behavior, it is clouding our vision and changing our behavior. Being in this world requires us to be tolerant and accepting of abnormal behavior that is contrary to biblical principles and teachings. The rampant growth of sin and our acute awareness of it is the consequence of the electronic age and the virtual revolution that has taken place over the last fifty years.

The real truth, though, is that we are in the Last Days, which means that, while Satan thinks that he has a hand in ruling this earth, his time is limited and his days are numbered! Jesus is soon coming again in accordance with the Scriptures, and the just on the earth will remain and rule the earth.

The Bible reminds us that in the last days, people will become wiser according to the world's standards, but weaker in faith. We see the evidence of that especially in America, where children seem to come out of the womb able to master current technology, while their parents are not training them up to seek the things of God anymore; as a result, their spirits are not being nurtured. Ephesians 6:4 states, "Fathers, do not exasperate your children; instead, bring them up in the training and instruction of the Lord." Proverbs 22:6 gives us another biblical mandate for raising children: "Start children off on the way they should

go, and even when they are old they will not turn from it." It's evident that God intended for Christian parents to make biblical and spiritual training a priority.

Parents take a tremendous risk when there is "no lifeguard on duty." Children under the age of eighteen should not be sent into the world without the teaching and knowledge of God and without adult supervision. We are in a cycle of change. Can children remain stable while the world's acceptance of unrighteousness is changing around them daily? The answer is *no*!

God's perspective has never changed. He is still the same yesterday, today, and forever. His expectations for Christians to live a Christ-like life have also not changed, regardless of what's happening in the world around us. We can see this very clearly in 2 Peter 1:3–11:

> *His divine power has given us everything we need for a godly life through our knowledge of him who called us by his own glory and goodness. Through these he has given us his very great and precious promises, so that through them you may participate in the divine nature, having escaped the corruption in the world caused by evil desires.*

For this very reason, make every effort to add to your faith goodness; and to goodness, knowledge; and to knowledge, self-control; and to self-control, perseverance; and to perseverance, godliness; and to godliness, mutual affection; and to mutual affection, love. For if you possess these qualities in increasing measure, they will keep you from being ineffective and unproductive in your knowledge of our Lord Jesus Christ. But whoever does not have them is nearsighted and blind, forgetting that they have been cleansed from their past sins.

Therefore, my brothers and sisters, make every effort to confirm your calling and election. For if you do these things, you will never stumble, and you will receive a rich welcome into the eternal kingdom of our Lord and Savior Jesus Christ.

We have a "helper" called the Holy Spirit that enables us to live up to God's expectations. Our reward here on earth is an abundant life, not without trials and tribulations, but with the loving support of a gracious God. We can do all things in Christ Jesus.

It's time for us to come out of the closet and raise the banner of Christ's truth in our world. God never meant for us to be a light hidden under a bush. We are the light of the world, and we have an obligation to be just that, with love. This directive does not require us to compromise our message in the middle of opposition, but to stand steadfast on God's Word and move according to the leading of the Holy Spirit. Your stance may not be popular, but it will be accurate.

Earlier, we talked about training children up in the things of God. That happens to be my purpose, and I've practiced it most of my life. As I walk the halls of schools nowadays, I see the blatant deterioration of the morals and biblical values that made this country into a great nation. It is the job of the Christian teacher to be that example in the schools across the nation. We are on stage, and our behavior influences the lives of children on a daily basis. This is the opportunity that we have to be a living testimony in a dark and dying world.

None of us are perfect, but if we live a surrendered life to Christ, then we are being perfected daily. Therein is the hope that we can emit our Christ-light before those who are stakeholders in our immediate spheres of influence.

Living a surrendered life to Christ also means listening to the Holy Spirit as He points out the sins that so easily

plague you—not only listening, but taking the necessary steps to rid yourself of anything that might hinder the fulfillment of your purpose in the assignment God has given you on earth. We glorify God in our weaknesses by loving Him enough to make the change. We also embrace the "tough love" that the Holy Spirit brings to our lives so that we can be more like Christ. Proverbs 12:1 states, "Whoever loves discipline loves knowledge, but whoever hates correction is stupid."

We also show the God kind of love to others when we are placed in a situation that requires us to love someone we perceive to be unlovable. Mark 12:33 compels us: "To love him [God] with all your heart, with all your understanding and with all your strength, and to love your neighbor as yourself is more important than all burnt offerings and sacrifices."

In conclusion, we are not in the world, we are not of the world, and we do whatever is necessary to glorify God by fulfilling His purpose for our lives. We must come out of our closets and be the disciples that we have been anointed to be and that the world needs.

PRAYER TO BE AN EFFECTIVE WITNESS FOR CHRIST

Heavenly Father, we bless Your holy name. You are so worthy to be glorified, and we give You all the honor and praise. I decree and declare that the Holy Spirit is my constant companion, and He reigns over my life as I walk on the paths of righteousness before You.

Renew my mind daily as I submit to Your command to draw all men to You. Help me, Lord, in my frailties to draw others into Your kingdom. You said that Your strength is made perfect in my weaknesses. Draw us by Your spirit out of the comfort of our closets to be the disciples that You have called us to be. Help us to possess the spiritual discipline that You have imparted to us in order to be effective witnesses on the earth. Help us to draw men, women, and children out of the control and dominion of Satan into Your marvelous light. May we do this all in honor of the sacrifice that Your Son made for us on Calvary, offering You and others the same love that took Jesus to the cross. In Jesus' name I pray, amen.

Chapter Eight Questions:

BEING IN THE WORLD AND NOT OF IT

1. What does being a heavenly ambassador for kingdom purpose mean to you?
2. What does being "in the world" look like from your perspective?
3. What does being "not of the world" look like from God's perspective?
4. How will you glorify God in your earthly witness and by fulfilling His purpose for your life?
5. How can you compromise your earthly witness of fulfilling God's purpose for your life?
6. Why are you, as a Christian, held to a higher standard than everyone else who has not professed Christianity?

CHAPTER 9

Modeling the Fruit of the Spirit in Your Life

"Likewise, teach the older women to be reverent in the way they live, not to be slanderers or addicted to much wine, but to teach what is good. Then they can urge the younger women to love their husbands and children, to be self-controlled and pure, to be busy at home, to be kind, and to be subject to their husbands, so that no one will malign the word of God." (Titus 2:3-5)

The Bible is the instruction manual for Christians. Its relevance supersedes the normalcy of the time we live in. The highest compliment that we can give to God is to model our lives based on biblical principles. Where do we find these principles? They are in the Bible. How will the unsaved find these principles? They get to witness your living testimony.

You mirror Christ by being faithful and true to your purpose. It's not something that you pick up and lay down; it really is something that requires a lifestyle and mindset change and a sincere effort to "walk the talk." One of God's most valuable assets is that He is so faithful to us. If we just mirror the asset of being faithful, we will see that our purpose will come to fruition. When we are on the stage of life, mirroring His faithfulness to others brings a sustaining power for our purpose-filled journey.

The foundation of Christ is one of love, and we have a responsibility to mirror love. Our actions must speak of the love of Christ. He must permeate everything we do for Him, especially in our interactions with others. How do we mirror His love? We consider others before ourselves. We sacrifice some of the things we need or want for the wellbeing of others.

Helping to assist and mentor others is something that we do out of our love for Christ. We also become a biblical role model out of our love for others to know Christ. Because God first loved us with an unconditional love, we should readily be willing to show it to others. I John 4:11 reminds us of the love mandate: "Dear friends, since God so loved us, we also ought to love one another." Joyce Meyer had this to say about love:

All the fruit of the Spirit are held in place by love. Jesus said that loving God and other people is the most important commandment. "You must love the LORD your God with all your heart, all your soul, and all your mind."[3] If you love others with that kind of love, there will be much fruit in your life.

Being Christ-like is the key to being a biblical role model. What tangible evidence could someone find in your life that would render you guilty of being Christ-like? With the measuring stick being the "fruits of the spirit," how do you measure up?

Here's a reminder of what the fruits are: But the fruit of the Spirit is love, joy, peace, forbearance, kindness, goodness, faithfulness, gentleness and self-control. Against such things there is no law"(Galatians 5:22–23).

Remember, these are the fruits of allowing yourself to be led by the Holy Spirit. These are not individual "fruits" that we get to pick and choose. The fruit of the Spirit is one nine-fold "fruit" that characterizes all who are led by the Holy Spirit. Collectively, these are the fruits that all Christians should be producing in their lives as "new creatures" in Jesus Christ.

---

3) *http://www.joycemeyer.org/articles/ea.aspx?article=fruit_of_the_spirit*

Below, I have provided an instructional nugget from the Bible for each "fruit" that comes from the Holy Spirit in our lives.

LOVE

1 John 4:16 says, "And so we know and rely on the love God has for us. God is love. Whoever lives in love lives in God, and God in them."

It has been my experience that this fruit is evident in your life when God has not only provided your needs, but also your wants. Because I have purposed in my life to live in the center of His will, He has rewarded me according to my faith and the fruit of my fulfilling His purpose for my life. Others have also sowed financially in my life because of the God kind of love that they possess.

Another way this fruit is evident in your life is when you are providing for someone else in their time of need and sacrificing a want so that you can help them. Becoming Christ to others in their time of need not only is an act of love but also increases the faith of its recipient. I remember distinctly our first lady calling for women who had a financial need to come to the front of the church. Once they arrived, she then asked that anyone being led to supply their needs to come up to the altar where the wom-

en were standing. There were three young women who came up to the front, and God spoke to me about the needs of one of them. I went up to her and whispered in her ear what the Holy Spirit told me. I shared with her what I was willing to do based on what the Holy Spirit had instructed me, and she cried. She had no idea that I knew what her need was, based on my conversation with the Holy Spirit. She needed her mortgage paid for that month. We left the sanctuary, went out into the corridor, and she gave me the short version of what she was going through. I wrote her the check, which was the outward demonstration of love.

I strongly believe that whatever you make happen for others, God makes happen for you. However, I also believe that you have an obligation to make whatever He has made happen for you happen for someone else. I remember very clearly when I was working on my doctorate and my husband was carrying the financial load for our family, we ended up on the foreclosure list three times. But God did not allow the bank to foreclose on our house because He always sent someone to meet our need. In like turn, this young lady knew God's glory because He physically demonstrated His love for her by answering her prayer

through me, an unsuspecting stranger. God got the glory based on what took place.

JOY

Nehemiah said, "Go and enjoy choice food and sweet drinks, and send some to those who have nothing prepared. This day is holy to our Lord. Do not grieve, for the joy of the Lord is your strength" (Nehemiah 8:10).

"The joy of the Lord is my strength" is a daily application for me. Each day that I awaken is a gift from God, so I wake up thanking Him and praising Him for life, health, and strength. His constant presence reminds me of the necessity to seek His joy with everything that I do during the day. Even in my weakness, I praise Him and depend on Him to strengthen me throughout the day.

PEACE

"Therefore, since we have been justified through faith, we have peace with God through our Lord Jesus Christ… "(Romans 5:1)

Without God there is no peace. If you have been employed for any length of time, you understand that there are days you find no peace. I have learned to walk in a room where there is utter chaos and declare God's peace

over my mind. I have also learned to declare the peace of God in the lives of others as they experience confusion. This is the same peace that Jesus walked in as He traveled to the cross.

FORBEARANCE *(LONGSUFFERING)*

Paul commands us in Ephesians 4:2: "Be completely humble and gentle; be patient, bearing with one another in love."

As Christians, we've got to go through some things. As a role model for others, people are not going to believe out story until they see the real you mirrored in that story. I could talk about longsuffering all day long to people that know me and know my character, but those outside of my immediate circle must see me going through it in order to really know my story. They must see my story lived out so that they can know God's glory through me.

KINDNESS

"We put no stumbling block in anyone's path, so that our ministry will not be discredited. Rather, as servants of God we commend ourselves in every way: in great endurance; in troubles, hardships and distresses; in beatings, imprisonments and riots; in hard work, sleepless nights and

hunger; in purity, understanding, patience and kindness; in the Holy Spirit and in sincere love..." (2 Corinthians 6:3–6)

Kindness is a virtue that we offer to others. The more you practice it, the more readily you are willing to share it because of the God-results you see manifested when you gift it to others. We do so because we are commanded to love others.

GOODNESS

"With this in mind, we constantly pray for you, that our God may make you worthy of his calling, and that by his power he may bring to fruition your every desire for goodness and your every deed prompted by faith." (2 Thessalonians 1:11)

Goodness comes from God. We must request it from Him, and once we receive it, we are empowered to perform our ministry calling and expect good results.

FAITHFULNESS

Paul said, "I thank Christ Jesus our Lord, who has strengthened me, because He considered me faithful, putting me into service..."(1 Timothy 1:12).

I learned faithfulness in my service as an educator. I am striving to hear, "Well done, you good and faithful servant" from God, as I fulfill my calling.

GENTLENESS *(MEEKNESS)*

"Brothers and sisters, if someone is caught in a sin, you who live by the Spirit should restore that person gently. But watch yourselves, or you also may be tempted."(Galatians 6:1)

Jesus had a very meek spirit. It was one of the qualities that drew people to Him. You can't lead people to Christ with a hearty stance. People want to see how genuine you are before they trust you or the God you are promoting.

SELF-CONTROL

"For this very reason, make every effort to add to your faith goodness; and to goodness, knowledge; and to knowledge, self-control; and to self-control, perseverance; and to perseverance, godliness; and to godliness, mutual affection; and to mutual affection, love." (2 Peter 1:5–7)

Self-control has been a definite virtue that has helped me succeed in life. I have purposed to live a life that is pleasing to God. I am human; therefore, I wrestle with

my flesh like everybody else, but what helps me is my deliberate attempt to live a disciplined life to glorify God.

Love for Christ compels us to fulfill His commandments. The lost were at the center of His missi on. Being a biblical role model requires a commitment not only to fulfilling your purpose, but also to being a true disciple of Christ. John 3:16 says, "For God so loved the world that he gave his one and only Son, that whoever believes in Him shall not perish but have eternal life." That requires an unconditional love, which Christ mirrored for us in His three years of ministry. Love will compel and equip you to fulfill your call to be a biblical role model. Simply accept the call because it pleases the Lover of your Soul!

PRAYER FOR INCREASING THE FRUIT OF THE SPIRIT IN YOUR LIFE

Father, I thank You for instructing me and teaching me about the fruit of the Spirit as I strive to practice each of them daily. Help me to continue on in my Christian walk as a biblical role model, reflecting Christ in all that I do. I purpose to walk by faith and not by sight. I will live a well-balanced and cautious life for You, Lord. I also purpose to have the mind of Christ Jesus and hold the thoughts, feelings, and purposes of His heart.

God, You have qualified and made me fit to share what I know about You in my Christian walk and while witnessing with others. You have translated me into the kingdom of Your dear Son. As I continue to know You better, You give me, through Your great power and authority, everything I need for this biblical role model assignment.

Thank You, Father, for the success You alone give to Your children while we strive to live a purpose-filled life.

In Jesus' name I pray, amen.

Chapter Nine Questions:

BEING A BIBLICAL ROLE MODEL

1. How should you mirror Christ in fulfilling your purpose?
2. What tangible evidence should someone be able to find in your Christian walk?   (i.e. fruit of the Spirit)
3. What biblical principles apply to this mandate?
4. Who has the authority to judge your progress?
5. How do you explain to a fallen world how your human fragility coexists with your superhuman ability to perform great exploits for God?

CHAPTER 10

Leaving a Purpose-Filled Legacy

"Then the eleven disciples went to Galilee, to the mountain where Jesus had told them to go. When they saw Him, they worshiped Him; but some doubted. Then Jesus came to them and said, 'All authority in heaven and on earth has been given to Me. Therefore go and make disciples of all nations, baptizing them in the name of the Father and of the Son and of the Holy Spirit, and teaching them to obey everything I have commanded you. And surely I am with you always, to the very end of the age.'" (Matthew 28:16–20)

Jesus left us a purpose-filled legacy in His short ministry which revolutionized the world. His willingness to fulfill His purpose, even until death, solidifies God's unquestionable love for us. What does your love toward

God and people compel you to leave for those who will come behind you?

Christ instructed His disciples to go out to the nations and duplicate themselves. We have an obligation to do the same, as we win others over to Christ. And it is important to the spiritual future of our descendants that we leave a purpose-filled legacy so that our lives will have meaning and relevance.

Are you living for just yourself, or are you living for those who will come behind you?

The answer you may give today is quite different from what you may have given over fifty years ago. In the world we live in, the common trend of thought is "I want mine, and I want it now." The problem with the twenty-first century adult is that we are not living for the generations that are coming behind us, and they know it.

The children today are a lot smarter street-wise than their Baby Boomer parents and grandparents, perhaps, but they are spiritually weaker. We must play to their strengths in order to be able to train them up in the things of God. It is critical that we find ways to bridge the generation gap and build up our children's spiritual muscles so that they will be able to fulfill their God-given destiny. As spiritual mentors, we must impart upon our youth the spiritual life lessons that we have learned about Christian living which they lack, in order for them to survive and thrive in this dark and dying world.

As an educator, I see the need every day in schools where I serve as a consultant. Many parents lack parenting skills, teachers have difficulty teaching, Christian disciples are not disciplining, and children are not growing in the things of God.

For some adults, you might have a similar experience as I did. Church was not optional in my life; I was exposed to the things of God at an early age, and gave my life to Christ at nine. I was raised in the fear and admonition of the Lord, and I gained an appreciation for the things of God that has sustained my life for over sixty years.

Unfortunately, often in our modern times, a lot of children aren't introduced to Christ and the benefits of serving Him early in life. If you are not exposed to Him, there's a good chance that you will spend your life seeking something to fill the hole in your heart or die with your purpose inside you. The world suffers as a result, and not only is your life-mission aborted, but those who were to benefit from it are severely influenced by its absence.

I am privileged to have many spiritual mentors, but there was one dynamic woman of God whose memory constantly acts as a plumb line for my purpose-centered mission, Dr. Alta Harvey.

I could not understand when Alta gave up her position at Region IV Education Service Center as a highly regarded Special Education Consultant to go work at our church. She had successfully completed her doctorate and was making good money in education at the time, but left to pursue her God-purpose. She took a serious cut in pay to work on staff as the Director of Christian Education Department. Being in the Church all of my life, I also understood how church people could be, which further complicated my understanding.

When she came to tell me that she was leaving, I was dumbfounded. However, as I got to know Alta's passion and understand the depth of her faith, I began to realize that she was merely walking according to God's purpose for her life.

I watched our church begin to blossom as she developed curriculum and set up effective Christian educational systems for discipleship. Her passion for mentoring women and equipping them for kingdom-purpose encouraged me to join her in this ministry and assist her. As a friend,

I remember her transparency, kindness, and boldness. Her humorous stories would have us laughing for days. She was not only a good friend, but also a visionary that understood the Great Commission and the key role Christian discipleship played within the walls of the church, as well as beyond. Thousands of lives were influenced by her obedience to God when He called her to fulltime ministry. Her name continues to resonate at Winsor Village United Methodist Church as the fruit of her ministry is evidenced in the lives of everyone that she touched.

There are also several biblical examples that were instrumental in my decision to leave a purpose-filled legacy. I was and still am reminded of Moses and how God saved him from imminent death as a baby. He was raised by Pharaoh's daughter and understood the protocols of Egypt. He ran away from the palace after he murdered an Egyptian soldier for striking one of his kinsmen, and stayed away for decades until God called him to fulfill his purpose-filled legacy of delivering His people and taking them to the Promised Land.

When he was first approached by God, Moses had numerous excuses for not feeling qualified to do the work of the Lord. You may be struggling also with your limitations,

but God would not have assigned you the task if He felt that you weren't qualified.

Sometimes we look at the situation with human eyes, and we see nothing but impossibilities. But God is able to do unimaginable things through us when we totally submit to His calling on our lives. We may look at the world around us and see the incomprehensible sin that is plaguing it, but we must not forget God has anointed us for His kingdom-purpose "for such a time as this" (Esther 4:14). Just as Moses triumphed over his infirmities and brought deliverance to others, so can you. You "can do all things through Christ who strengthens you" (Phil. 4:14).

Another example I look to is Rahab, the prostitute that made a choice to follow the dictates of her conscience and hide the spies from Israel in her home when they were exposed in foreign territory. This woman of God is listed in Hebrews 11, in the "Faith Hall of Fame," among those men and women who had great faith. Joshua spared Rahab and her family because of her act of bravery, and she ended up marrying into the direct bloodline of Jesus Christ.

Paul's account of his life is the plumb line that I use as my own standard. He states:

> *But I do not consider my life of any account*
> *as dear to myself, into order that I may finish*

my course, and the ministry which I received
from the Lord Jesus, to testify solemnly of the
gospel of the grace of God." (Acts 20:24)

This book is a part of my legacy for fellow believers and those who are seeking to live according to God's purpose. I also serve wholeheartedly in my local ministry, and I have purposed to leave this kind of legacy in my life to the students, parents, and administrators that I serve through my business by taking Christ with me wherever I go. I have been deliberate about leaving a spiritual legacy for my child and grandchildren by being a biblical role model and truly training them in the things of God. This is all a part of my Great Commission mandate.

Let's take a look at some Scriptures that support the idea of leaving a purpose-filled legacy in order to fulfill the Great Commission that Jesus left His disciples:

"And He said to them, 'Go into all the world
and preach the gospel to all creation.'"
(Mark 16:15)

"…and that repentance for forgiveness of sins
should be proclaimed in His name to all the
nations, beginning from Jerusalem."
(Luke 24:47)

"Jesus therefore said to them again, 'Peace be with you; as the Father has sent Me, I also send you.'" (John 20:21)

"When I [the Lord] say to the wicked, 'You shall surely die'; and you do not warn him or speak out to warn the wicked from his wicked way that he may live, that wicked man shall die in his iniquity, but his blood I will require at your hand." (Ezekiel 3:18)

"Now all these things are from God, who reconciled us to Himself through Christ, and gave us the ministry of reconciliation..."
(2 Corinthians 5:18)

"And working together with Him [God], we also urge you not to receive the grace of God in vain..." (2 Corinthians 6:1)

"Therefore, we are ambassadors for Christ, as though God were entreating through us; we beg you on behalf of Christ, be reconciled to God." (2 Corinthians 5:20)

"And there is salvation in no one else; for there is no other name under heaven that has been given among men, by which we must be saved." (Acts 4:12)

"We must work the works of Him who sent Me [Christ], as long as it is day; night is coming, when no man can work." (John 9:4)

"He said to them, 'It is not for you to know times or epochs which the Father has fixed by His own authority; but you shall receive power when the Holy Spirit has come upon you; and you shall be My witnesses both in Jerusalem, and in all Judea and Samaria, and even to the remotest part of the earth.'" (Acts 1:7–8)

"And this gospel of the kingdom shall be preached in the whole world for a witness to all the nations, and then the end shall come." (Mat 24:14)

These are tools that lay the precedence for your end time ministry. Learn them well, and then set about to do them.

PRAYER FOR LEAVING A PURPOSE-FILLED LEGACY

Dear Heavenly Father, King of all nations, who reigns in heaven and in my heart, holy is your name. I stand in agreement with You that Your will be done in my life as You purposed it before I was formed in my mother's womb. Help me to live a life of purpose for others and not just for myself. Help me to live so that I can leave a purpose-filled legacy for those who will come behind me in my family, my church, and my community. I purposely model my life after the life of Christ in hope that I will be a light reflecting Your love in a loveless world.

Forgive me for being selfish, only living for my needs and not considering the needs of others. I purpose in my walk to reach the mark of the high calling that You have placed on my life, and to do it for the glory of Your kingdom.

In Jesus' name I pray, amen.

Chapter Ten Questions:

LEAVING A PURPOSE-FILLED LEGACY

1. Why is it important to leave a purpose-filled legacy for those who will come behind us?
2. Who left a purpose-filled legacy for you?
3. What biblical or present examples come to mind when you think about leaving a purpose filled legacy?
4. How have you purposed to leave this kind of legacy for others?
5. What other Scriptures support leaving a purpose-filled legacy for fulfilling the Great Commission?

CHAPTER 11

Don't Give Up

*"Let us not become weary in doing good,
for at the proper time we will reap a harvest if we
do not give up." (Galatians 6:9)*

Always act like the person you believe you are in Christ. Failure to do so can abort your purpose. "As a man thinketh," Proverbs 23:7 says, "so he is…" Know that God sometimes brings our provision through people that we are ready to give up on. Do not give up so soon that it causes you to miss your blessing. Your Godly rewards are in your ability to differentiate what is God and what is not.

Find someone with an unhappy countenance, and you will find a person who has given up on pursuing their purpose. It is all a matter of your perspective. Do not base

your attitude on your present situation. Rejoice in the Lord! Your perspective and attitude should elevate you to God's higher perspective. Wait on His cue, and know that you will reach your destined purpose with new power!

A lot of Christians give up pursing their purpose based on a lack of confidence that they are moving in the right direction. Some even lack confidence in themselves that they can't do what they resolve to do. They have forgotten that all of our strength comes from God. When you really trust Him and follow His leadership, and you get to that point where you find yourself moving in the wrong direction, connect with Him through prayer. Praying keeps you on the right road.

Christians, like everyone else, get distracted. There are so many things going on around you, or within you that can distract you. Things going on in your family or in your everyday world can keep us away from pursuing our purpose. Christians also, whether they admit it or not, get tired of doing the right thing, especially if they are looking at others around them who seem to be blessed when they are not doing the right thing, while the Christian is tirelessly pursuing their purpose and trying to move forward in that direction despite heavy opposition. It is only natural to get very tired of seeing the "bad guy" win all the time.

We give up and miss out on the fruits of our labor due to our lack of understanding others or not being in the right place at the right time. But your problems are often what serve as promotions into your destined future!

When you give up, you miss out on the blessings that God has in store for you. You miss out on God's perfect plan that He has for you. You lose your available resources in God, who is your divine resource for all things. It's critical that you do not forget from where your strength comes, the good that comes out while fulfilling your purpose, and that *He* is your resource. Remember, "All things work together for good to them that love God…" (Romans 8:28). That is why it is so critical for us not to give up. It's not just about you; it's about people, processes, and situations that are out there depending on you to fulfill your purpose so that the next generation can be better.

The first and foremost benefit of not giving up on fulfilling your purpose, however is that you have lived a life pleasing to God. When you make Him and fulfilling His purpose the priority in your life, you know that you have a heavenly home awaiting you with eternal life.

The second benefit is that there are so many people depending on you to be successful in pursuing your pur-

pose. Know that the whole idea of others being blessed by your obedience gives you an incredible sense of accomplishment and satisfaction.

The third benefit is knowing that Jesus showed His love for us by dying on the cross; so, if He gave us that sacrifice of unimaginable love, then we as His children get an opportunity to emulate that love in doing the same while fulfilling our purpose.

The most meaningful loss for you by not fulfilling your purpose is the unspeakable joy that you give up as a result of not completing your heavenly mission. In fulfilling God's destined purpose for your life, there is so much joy in the tasks that you do for others. The sacrifices that you seemingly endure in the eyes of others make you a Christian billboard of faith, providing you with so much joy. You lose that joy when you are not operating in God's purpose.

There is also the fascinating big picture that you are able to see, demonstrating how God is moving the small pieces of that puzzle together for your life. The whole idea of who you are comes into full manifestation when you are pursuing your purpose. You begin to see in fullness the Master Creator's plan for your life, and you are amazed by His ability to do a perfect work in you that benefits not only your life, but that of others.

We are unlike everyone around us. We must understand that the significance of what happens while we are moving toward our purpose is what we experience in our relationship with the Lord on the way there. Who and what you are become essential to His plan for your life. We must strive to persevere through the hardships of life so that we may do His will and be rewarded with a purpose-filled life.

Some of my favorite biblical examples of perseverance are Hezekiah and John the Baptist. Isaiah 38:1–7 tells Hezekiah's story:

> *In those days Hezekiah became ill and was at the point of death. The prophet Isaiah son of Amoz went to him and said, "This is what the Lord says: 'Put your house in order, because you are going to die; you will not recover.'" Hezekiah turned his face to the wall and prayed to the Lord, "Remember, Lord, how I have walked before you faithfully and with wholehearted devotion and have done what is good in your eyes." And Hezekiah wept bitterly. Then the word of the Lord came to Isaiah: "Go and tell Hezekiah, 'This is what the Lord, the God of your father David, says: "I have heard your prayer and seen your tears;*

> *I will add fifteen years to your life. And I will*
> *deliver you and this city from the hand of the*
> *king of Assyria. I will defend this city. This is the*
> *Lord's sign to you that the Lord will do what he*
> *has promised..."''*

The whole idea of getting close to and walking in your purpose relies on your ability to pray. I don't mean an ability based on your intellectual or good-works capacity, but a spiritual ability to get a prayer through to the Most High God. Hezekiah turned his face to the wall, eliminating all distractions, and petitioned God for as long as it took for God to change His mind. This was done so that Hezekiah's purpose would be fulfilled and the city rescued.

Now let's take a look at John the Baptist:

> *Now Herod had arrested John and bound him*
> *and put him in prison because of Herodias, his*
> *brother Philip's wife, for John had been saying*
> *to him: "It is not lawful for you to have her."*
> *Herod wanted to kill John, but he was afraid*
> *of the people, because they considered John*
> *a prophet.*
> *On Herod's birthday the daughter of Herodias*
> *danced for the guests and pleased Herod so*

*much that he promised with an oath to give
her whatever she asked. Prompted by her
mother, she said, "Give me here on a platter
the head of John the Baptist." The king was
distressed, but because of his oaths and his
dinner guests, he ordered that her request
be granted and had John beheaded in the
prison. His head was brought in on a platter
and given to the girl, who carried it to her
mother. John's disciples came and took his
body and buried it. Then they went and told
Jesus. (Matthew 14:3–12)*

John the Baptist stayed his course and did all that God required of him, even to the point of being beheaded. Being persistent in your calling sometimes takes you to unfamiliar places and difficult situations. John the Baptist was born to prepare the way for Jesus. He stood for righteousness, even to the point where he riled Herod and his queen, who was previously his brother's wife. We know the end of the story, but John's blood was not shed before he had completed the call of God on his life—which was to declare Jesus' coming and condemn Herod's sin.

We often think we are sacrificing a lot when we answer the call of God on our lives. We hesitate like the young rich ruler to leave our material possessions and position of power behind, but John did not. Even though God rarely calls us to give up our lives to the point of death, we often cry, complain, and mourn over the things that He has asked us to step away from in order to fulfill His purpose for our lives. What God is asking us to do is absolutely nothing in comparison to what He has required of us.

We are all passing through this life, and we only have one life to give to God. If you really want to be engaged in the blessings that God has in store for you, you've got to have an attitude of persistence, prayer, and belief that God is your resource. He may send people or things to help you, but if you really are depending on God, there is no reason to give up. If you do give up for a day, that doesn't mean that He has given up on you. Reconnect to your heavenly power source, the Holy Spirit, and get back on track. Let us "not become weary in doing good, for at the proper time we will reap a harvest if we do not give up" (Galatians 6:9).

Don't give up, for "the vision is yet for an appointed time, but at the end it shall speak and not lie. Though it tarry, wait for it, because it will surely come; it will not tarry" (Habakkuk 2:3).

PRAYER FOR NOT GIVING UP

Sustaining God, the Almighty Creator and Prince of Peace, Your fullness abides in me. You lead me and carry me day by day. In difficult times, I will rest in You and wait patiently for Your instructions. Your perspective on life is above my comprehension. I won't give up on You or Your sustaining power as I pursue Your purpose for my life. As I think, so I am. Therefore, the joy of the Lord is my strength. The peace of the Lord surpasses understanding. You are my deliverer, so I will not give up. I will forgive and be forgiven. I will love and be loved, because I can do all things in You, oh Lord.

In Jesus' name I pray, Amen.

Chapter Eleven Questions :

DON'T GIVE UP

1. What are some of the reasons that Christians give up on pursuing their purpose?
2. Why is it critical for you not to give up?
3. What are the benefits from not giving up on living your life according to His purpose?
4. What do you lose when you don't fulfill your God-given purpose?
5. What biblical and present role models would you reference for showing persistence in pursuit of their purpose?

CHAPTER 12

Walking in the Fullness of God's Purpose

"I can do all this through him who gives me strength."
(Philippians 4:13)

As Christians, walking in the fullness of God's purpose is our true destination. If you are a seasoned Christian, you understand the importance of finishing your race. You are prepared to make a proclamation at the end of this faith journey similar to the apostle Paul's:"I have fought the good fight, I have finished the race, I have kept the faith" (2 Timothy 4:7).

If you are a Christian novice, you may be asking yourself what walking in the fullness of God's purpose looks like, wondering how you will know when you've completed your mission.

Walking in the fullness of God's purpose means living the best life that you possibly can with and for God. Your best life is a life that is totally surrendered to God.

First, you must accept Christ as your Lord and Savior, and as the head of your life. Then, you must repent and seek the heart of God to discover the Christian tenets that are specific to your calling. God made you unique in order to fulfill your specific calling. Thus, He will equip you to accomplish the task at hand. Seeking Him for those tools which will render you successful is part of your duty as a Christian who is bent on serving God and fulfilling your earthly mission. You are destined to do "great" things for God simply because *He* is a great God.

In an earlier chapter, we discussed the fruit of the Spirit (love, joy, peace, patience, kindness, goodness, faithfulness, gentleness, and self-control). You will know that you are walking in the fullness of God's purpose when there is evidence of those fruit on your spiritual tree. Psalm 1:3 puts it like this:"That person is like a tree planted by streams of water, which yields its fruit in season and whose leaf does not wither—whatever they do prospers."It is a wonderful place to be where whatever you do for the Lord brings prosperity into your life. If you want to improve the overflow of blessing of your life, make walking in the full-

ness of your purpose a priority, and watch out for God's blessings.

Others will also know that you are walking according to God's purpose when they see you exhibit those fruit, regardless of the season of life you are in. A tree experiences good and bad weather, but its foundation determines its longevity. If its roots are anchored in good soil, it can last many lifetimes. If you are anchored in God, walking in the fullness of your purpose will be your pleasure, and the fruit of your Godly attitude will be proof of your durability. When the trials of life come your way, stress will not be your body's response. You will also walk in an uncommon personal satisfaction when achieving your purpose that supersedes one's expectation.

Another fruit you will see is that you will be in a better position to make good decisions about your life, because your mind is aligned with your God-purpose. The practical Christian should desire this fruit because it benefits everyone from their family to those they serve in their ministry, on the job, or as an entrepreneur. These additional fruits are the byproduct of walking in the fullness of God's presence.

Contrary to the opinion of the world, the Christian life is an enjoyable one, filled with the goodness and riches of God. In your submission, He shapes you to fit the divine calling on your life for true victory. For example, looking from the outside in at the horrific betrayal and death of Jesus Christ, one may lose all hope, like His disciples. However, when you consider the God-factor in Christ's death, He was crucified yes, but He was also resurrected and ascended to the right hand of God the Father, where He is currently interceding for us daily. He uses the same power to resurrect us into our glorious purpose when we leave the ways of the world for the glory of a kingdom lifestyle.

Walking in the fullness of your purpose is also knowing that when you face the trials and tribulations of life, you are equipped to win the battle. Satan does all that he can to deter you from it, but God has supernaturally equipped you for success. Once you realize that, you are energized to completion. In other words, God makes you a finisher.

You will know that you are in your purpose when you are really *living* and not just "existing." The joy of the Lord will be your constant companion. Your spirit-man will bear witness with the Holy Spirit, and He will fill you with the sustaining power and peace of God that makes you an overcomer in all situations. When Paul and Silas were in

prison, for example, it was obvious that the joy of the Lord was their strength.

Let's take a look at the story in Acts 16:25-28:

> *About midnight Paul and Silas were praying and singing hymns to God, and the other prisoners were listening to them. Suddenly there was such a violent earthquake that the foundations of the prison were shaken. At once all the prison doors flew open, and everyone's chains came loose. The jailer woke up, and when he saw the prison doors open, he drew his sword and was about to kill himself because he thought the prisoners had escaped. But Paul shouted, "Don't harm yourself! We are all here!"*

Paul and Silas purposed to please God by worshiping Him, and they were literally set free from prison. And not only were they set free, but all of the other prisoners were, too!

What this shows us is that another key factor to look for when you are walking in your purpose is its effect on the lives of others.

There is an unexplainable joy and sense of completion that you get when you see the God-result of your efforts when serving others. Just like Paul and Silas had a profound effect on the life of the jailer, you can also see that manifested in the lives of those that God has called you to minister to.

Walking in the fullness of your purpose is not about constantly asking God to bless you. The proof that you are living purpose-filled is when you can look around and see that others are better off having known you or having been in your presence. Walking in the fullness of your purpose is when your children or grandchildren look up to you and say that you are blessed, like the Proverbs 31 woman: "Her children arise and call her blessed; her husband also, and he praises her: 'Many women do noble things, but you surpass them all'" (v.29).

At my husband's funeral several years ago, our pastor spoke some powerful words into my DNA. He said, "Gene and Jackie make a difference, and a Proverbs Woman and a Proverbs Man go around making a difference." I will never forget that statement. Our true testimony was that my husband and I were making an evident difference in the lives of others because we purposed to walk in the fullness of God's calling on our lives. I have sown my life into the public educational system, and he sowed his life into public service as a labor union representative. When God joined us together, little did I know that we would be a force used for His glory. But through the mentorship of the Holy Spirit, we grew as a blended family to a point in our walks where we were able to be philanthropists and serve others so that they could fulfill their God-purpose through various ministries at and beyond our local church. I can say with the utmost confidence that God was good to us as a married couple, and is still good to me as a result.

Others will know you as a witness for Christ when you walk in humility. You are consistent in your faith walk when you perform the menial tasks that others will not want to do or walk the narrow road that others refuse to walk on. They will know that you are purpose-driven when your "haters" talk about you and those listening say, "That's not the person I know." People will know that you are fulfilling your purpose when they see you doing what God expects you to do. They will know that you are mission-minded when they see your miraculous favor in accomplishing tasks that were unimaginable. Still others will know that we are walking in our purpose when we are rewarded and recognized for our faithfulness.

It has taken a lifetime of experiences to develop a true foundation for this book. However, following that major car accident which nearly took my life, I have used the time while healing to pen the finishing touches of it. It is my best rendering orchestrated by the Holy Spirit. My prayer is that it has been beneficial and encouraging to you to walk *According to His Purpose*.

We are all equipped for service to build up the body of Christ. We are ambassadors from a heavenly kingdom in a dark and dying world. When the body collectively pursues their God-given purpose, the result is a mature Church operating under the divine direction of Jesus Christ. Ephesians 4:11–13 states the Church's purpose:

> *So Christ Himself gave the apostles, the prophets, the evangelists, the pastors and teachers, to equip His people for works of service, so that the body of Christ may be built up until we all reach unity in the faith and in the knowledge of the Son of God and become mature, attaining to the whole measure of the fullness of Christ.*

Our goal then, is that we become more Christ-like and get the results He desired for us on the earth, fulfilling

the Great Commission mandate and making disciples in every nation.

Walking in the fullness of your calling qualifies you to fulfill this mandate *According to His Purpose*.

To God Be the Glory.

PRAYER TO WALK ACCORDING TO HIS PURPOSE

Lord God, Your Word says that I can do all things through Christ who strengthens me. I stand on Your Word as I walk in the fullness of Your purpose for my life. I will finish each race stronger and more convinced of Your power working in me.

Father, help me to demonstrate the fruit of the Spirit: love, joy, peace, patience, kindness, goodness, faithfulness, gentleness, and self-control. Anchor me in Your love. Your love conquers everything.

Forgive me for not accepting the assignment of fulfilling the purpose You placed on my life, as I forgive those who blocked me along the way. Lead me away from the evil one. I will walk in the fullness of God's purpose for my life and be a role model for others. I will bring You the glory due Your name.

In Jesus' name I pray, amen.

Chapter Twelve Questions:

WALKING IN THE FULLNESS OF GOD'S PURPOSE

1. What does walking in the fullness of God's purpose look like?
2. How will you know when you are there?
3. How will others know when you are there?
4. How will you measure the impact that spiritual knowledge and intellectual knowledge have made on your life?
5. How will you measure your success in walking according to God's purpose?

ABOUT the AUTHOR

Dr. Jacqueline Horton-Cobbin has a unique way of reaching her audience by coining phrases called "Cobbinisms". These phrases are "You are always on stage. Treat people as you want to be treated. There is no substitute for documentation. And with spiritual and intellectual knowledge, you are a powerful individual." This is the basis by which she has thrived as a multidimensional entrepreneur leader, professional educator, gifted communicator and philanthropist. She is a nationally recognized presenter and motivational speaker and known as "one of the most effective and results-oriented consultants in America."

As CEO of Cobbin & Associates, LLC, Dr. Cobbin has served as an educational consultant, technical writer and editor for non-profit and profit organizations, edu-

cational institutions, as well as for church leaders for over 10 years. She has also released several audio teachings, "How Will You Live Your Life When No One Else Is Watching?"; "You Are What You Write"; and a video library "Parent Power and The Power of Prayer." Aspiring to make a greater impact on others, mentoring young women and girls and expanding her God-given kingdom authority while leaving a purpose driven legacy is Cobbin's calling.

Made in the USA
Monee, IL
23 September 2023